the new crewel

the new crewel

Exquisite Designs in Contemporary Embroidery

Katherine Shaughnessy

LARK BOOKS

A Division of Sterling Publishing Co., Inc.
New York

Editor: ELAINE LIPSON

Art Director: DANA IRWIN

Cover Designer:
BARBARA ZARETSKY

Photographer: STEVE MANN

Illustrator: OLIVIER ROLLIN

Assistant Editor:
REBECCA GUTHRIE

Assistant Art Director:
LANCE WILLE

Associate Art Director:
SHANNON YOKELEY

Editorial Assistance:
DELORES GOSNELL

Editorial Intern:
DAVID SQUIRES

Library of Congress Cataloging-in-Publication Data

Shaughnessy, Katherine, 1970-
  The new crewel : exquisite designs in contemporary embroidery / Katherine
Shaughnessy.
      p. cm.
  Includes bibliographical references and index.
  ISBN 1-57990-680-X (pbk.)
  1. Crewelwork—Patterns. I. Title.
TT778.C7S53 2005
746.44'6041—dc22

                                    2005012492

10 9 8 7 6 5 4 3 2

Published by Lark Books, A Division of
Sterling Publishing Co., Inc.
387 Park Avenue South, New York, N.Y. 10016

Text © 2005, Katherine Shaughnessy
Photography and illustrations © 2005, Lark Books

Distributed in Canada by Sterling Publishing,
c/o Canadian Manda Group, 165 Dufferin Street
Toronto, Ontario, Canada M6K 3H6

Distributed in the United Kingdom by GMC Distribution Services,
Castle Place, 166 High Street, Lewes, East Sussex, England BN7 1XU

Distributed in Australia by Capricorn Link (Australia) Pty Ltd.,
P.O. Box 704, Windsor, NSW 2756 Australia

If you have questions or comments about this book, please contact:
Lark Books
67 Broadway, Asheville, NC 28801
(828) 253-0467

Manufactured in China

ISBN 13: 978-1-57990-680-1
ISBN 10: 1-57990-680-X

For information about custom editions, special sales, premium and corporate purchases, please contact Sterling Special Sales Department at 800-805-5489 or specialsales@sterlingpub.com.

DEDICATION

To the next generation

Katherine Shaughnessy was born in 1970 in Lakewood, Ohio. At an early age she learned to use a needle and thread with the help of crewel kits given to her by her mother. She's been sewing ever since, making everything from custom drapery and embroidered pillow cases to stitched greeting cards and silk wedding dresses. In 1992, Katherine received a BFA from Miami University, where her hand sewing found its way into both her paintings and sculptures. She continued her study of the fine arts as a graduate student in the Fiber Department at the School of the Art Institute of Chicago, where she received an MFA in 1997. From her home in the mountains of far west Texas, Katherine is still making sculptures and paintings with a strong emphasis in stitching and the fiber arts. In 2003, she began developing contemporary designs for her crewel embroidery kits, which she launched in 2004 under the company name Wool & Hoop. Katherine is on a mission to bring crewel embroidery back to life as a way to teach both young and old the needle arts. Her crewel kits are available on the internet at woolandhoop.com and at more than 50 stores throughout the U.S., U.K, and Canada.

CONTENTS

INTRODUCTION

WELCOME TO THE NEW CREWEL

■ With this book, I hope to honor the old and celebrate the new, weaving the traditional crewelwork methods and materials of the past with the modern sensibilities and design elements of today.

Crewel is a form of embroidery that uses two-ply worsted wool threads on linen fabric. If you've ever embroidered, you're a step ahead, because crewelwork uses traditional embroidery stitches known around the world. If you're a knitter, you'll be right at home with the thick wool threads, and will appreciate the contrast of their luscious texture on bright linen twill. If you're an artist, you'll see the unlimited possibilities of "painting" with vibrant crewel wools and "sculpting" with dimensional crewel stitches. If you're an experienced creweler, just looking for something different, you'll welcome this whole new approach to crewel design—what I call "The New Crewel" (also, of course, the name of this book!).

And finally, if you've never picked up a needle and thread, this is a perfect time and place to begin. There was a day when decorative embroidery, and crewelwork specifically, was the first exposure a young person had to stitching. (I was lucky enough to be introduced to crewelwork when I was just five years old, and have been a lover of the fiber arts ever since.) So welcome—young or old, experienced or not—to The New Crewel.

Some dedicated crewel embroiderers have been creweling since the 1960s and '70s, when fabric stores carried an abundance of crewel kits. Those were the days when designs in the style of classic Jacobean embroidery still shared shelf space with cutesy, campy animal designs in earth-tone colors. Sadly, since then, whole generations of crafters have never even heard of crewel.

Today is a turning point for crewel embroidery. The New Crewel of the 21st century aims to insure that no more generations of would-be crewelers are lost due to lack of exposure to the craft, or because they see only outdated designs. With this book, I hope to give needle artists and crafters alike a reason to return to, or try for the first time, the rich wools and pure linens of crewel embroidery.

The New Crewel's organization easily lends itself to helping both inexperienced and experienced embroiderers. I've offered a brief history, with three well-known examples of crewelwork from previous times. The materials and tools needed for the craft are explained in-depth, as are the essential techniques necessary to get started. You'll also find a helpful gallery of 16 stitches, with easy-to-follow instructions. Though there are hundreds of crewel embroidery stitches, these basic stitches are demonstrated at least once throughout the book's projects, giving you plenty of opportunities to practice with your favorites.

What makes this book unique is its gallery of 30 original designs. After learning to stitch the basic patterns, feel free to explore the simple projects. Think of the greeting card, sachet, lampshade, and others as starting points for your own creative ideas. Once you free your imagination, you'll find so many ways to include crewel embroidery on wearables and home accents.

A BRIEF HISTORY OF CREWELWORK

■ To get a sense of where we are today, we need to understand where we were yesterday, so let's begin with a little history.

The threads of embroidery run deep into the Middle Ages. The best-known medieval work is the *Bayeux Tapestry,* a 231-foot-long embroidery in worsted wool on linen fabric that depicts the Norman Conquest of 1066. Crewelwork really came of age a bit later, in early 17th century England. This was the golden age of crewel. British sea merchants were bringing embroidery from India, and local manufacturers began forging steel sewing needles. Because the name of the king at that time was James I (Jacobus, in Latin), we call it Jacobean embroidery. English embroiderers were busy creating what has become classic crewel: flowers, birds, the tree of life, and other scenes from nature. Their crewel stitches are still in use today.

Jacobean crewelwork wasn't confined to Great Britain. It skipped across the sea to the early American colonies. There, crewel circulated among well-to-do women, on petticoat borders coyly peeking out from beneath long skirts, or on elaborate covers for canopy beds.

The rage faded, though, and crewel pretty much sat out the 18th century, as other needlework and fabrics came into fashion. But by the 1820s, a new style of wool embroidery, called Berlin woolwork, became extremely popular in England and America, and was widely practiced for decades. Berlin woolwork was like modern-day

cross-stitch or needlepoint, with similar stitches, gridlike patterns, and a bright, "anything goes" color palette. Though its repetitive patterns may seem uninspiring, Berlin woolwork kept society women in stitches into the mid-19th century.

However, the next few decades brought a big change. Embroidery with wool reached a watershed moment in the late 19th century, in the hands of a new wave of artists. These historical hipsters were far-sighted: they took ideas, not just from the previous generation, but also from other disciplines such as painting, architecture, philosophy, and history.

English designer William Morris was one of their leading lights. A few centuries earlier, they would have called him a Renaissance man. A few centuries later, he'd have been labeled multi-disciplinary. But there was no doubt that William Morris was your classic do-it-yourself crafter. His DIY ethos brought him to every aspect of

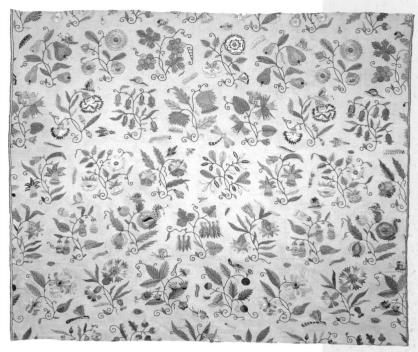

interior design—furniture, wallpaper, stained glass, carpets—and even into poetry and politics. He formed a group of like-minded artists in the 1860s and dove into the decorative arts, creating embroideries, tapestries, church windows, and what his contemporary, the painter and poet Dante Gabriel Rossetti, called "some intensely medieval furniture."

When Morris moved into a new house, he was disappointed that he couldn't find anything in the stores to help him deck it out. So he decided to do it himself, with homemade furniture and

Embroidery. England, James I period, early 17th c. Embroidery, silk, 66.04 x 76.20 cm. ©The Cleveland Museum of Art, Purchase from the J.H. Wade Fund, 1933.421

embroideries (see example on page 13). Pretty soon the whole family, including his wife and children, were doing crewelwork. The Morris family motto, sometimes stitched into his embroideries, was "If I Can."

The catch-all name given to this new type of sewing was Art Needlework, and crewel was its most popular form. Whereas Berlin woolwork was seen as an everyday hobby, this new crewel craze was elevated to an art form. Finally, the "decorative arts" were getting emphasis on the second word.

"STUDY OLD WORK TO SEE WHAT HAS BEEN DONE, AND HOW IT HAS BEEN DONE, AND THEN DO ONE'S OWN IN ONE'S OWN WAY."

There was a coolness to the colors used in Art Needlework. Its minimalism contrasted with the gaudiness of Berlin woolwork. A writer in a British magazine of 1886 observed that the crewel craze "should do much to lift the art of embroidery out of that horrible fancy needlework and teapot-cozy groove into which, in the hands of Philistines, it is so apt to fall."

Crewelwork was gaining an audience, and in the 1870s it hit the big time with the establishment of the Royal School of Art Needlework in the Kensington borough of London. The school, which is still in operation today, was so influential that the crewel embroidery stitch that we know as Split Stitch came to be called the Kensington Stitch or the Kensington Outline Stitch in the United States.

Art Needlework was part of the broader Arts and Crafts Movement. It was taught by skilled artists who encouraged student crafters, in the words of Lewis F. Day, a designer and author of the time, to "study old work to see what has been done, and how it has been done, and then do one's own in one's own way." It was this emphasis on new designs with a respect and understanding of art history that made the crewel movement of the 1870s so successful.

In the years that followed, crewelwork, like all the handmade arts, withstood the challenges of increased mechanization, as cheaply printed, decorative textiles flooded the market. Still, every era had its handmaidens of the handmade. The Arts and Crafts movement, for example, was in part a response to the Industrial Revolution. And 100 years later, in the 1960s and '70s, another resurgence of crewel began in Britain and the United States.

Excellent designers guided this crewel revival, just as others had done before. One of the best was Erica Wilson, a skilled teacher of crewel who was educated at the Royal School of Needlework in London. Wilson's instructional crewel books, showcasing her intricate, Jacobean-influenced designs,

Crewel embroidery from a store-bought kit, Katherine Shaughnessy, 1979. Crewel wool embroidered on linen, including Chain, Satin, Stem, and Spiderweb Stitches

continue to inspire crewelers today. Still, the crewel world steadily lost population in the closing decades of the 20th century.

With this book, I hope to offer a chance for a renewed understanding and appreciation of traditional hand embroidery, along with the inspiration to create unique and contemporary crewel designs. Good creweling, crafters!

Wall Hanging,
William Morris, 1877. T.166-1978. Crewel wool embroidered on linen with Stem, Satin Stitches, and French Knots. 207.5 x 153 cm. ©V&A Images

Embroidery,
Erica Wilson, Cover art from her book, **Crewel Embroidery,** first published in 1962

THE NEW CREWEL BASICS

MATERIALS

You will need to obtain a number of basic supplies in order to enjoy crewel. This section describes the materials you can find in craft and needlework stores.

LINEN TWILL

Linen twill is the traditional fabric base for crewelwork. Linen is a very sturdy, natural material. When woven in a twill pattern, it does not have the gridlike system of holes seen in the plain weave fabrics of needlepoint and cross-stitch (fig. 1). The tight, smooth, and uninterrupted surface of a twill weave is perfect for the freeform style of crewel embroidery (fig. 2).

Many needlecraft shops and online stores specializing in embroidery supplies carry linen twills specifically for crewelwork, in either 100 percent linen or a linen blend. Most come in white or off-white, but can be easily colored before being embroidered by using fabric

dyes available at most craft stores and drugstores. All of the designs in this book were done on white linen twill found at an embroidery supply shop.

Having just said that linen twill is the traditional fabric for crewelwork, sometimes I can't help breaking the rules. In some of the projects in this book, I used materials other than linen, including polyester fleece and cotton blue jeans. Just remember that the wool thread you'll be stitching with tends to shrink. Therefore, your projects, whether done on linen twill or polyester fleece, must either be dry-cleaned, or carefully hand-washed in cold water and air-dried.

CREWEL WOOL THREAD

The thread, or yarn, used in crewel embroidery is loosely twisted two-ply worsted wool. The wool is not soft and fuzzy like knitting yarn. Worsted wool comes from long-haired English sheep, and is combed and

Plain Weave
Figure 1

Twill Weave
Figure 2

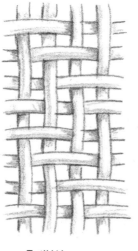

Knitting Yarn   Worsted Wool   Two-Ply Worsted
Figure 3

spun until it is smooth like a rope. Two strands of this worsted wool are then loosely twisted together ("two-ply") to make crewel wool thread (fig. 3).

Most needlecraft shops and online stores carry several brands of crewel wool thread. Hundreds of colors are available, allowing for both dramatic and subtle color changes, similar to a painter's palette. Crewel wool is usually sold by the hank, a fairly large quantity, or by the skein, a smaller quantity. For the projects in this book, buy your wool in skeins.

Because crewel wool thread is not very strong, you should use thread no longer than 14 inches (35.5 cm) when doing crewelwork. As you work, begin a new piece of thread as soon as the one you're working with begins to wear out.

Tapestry wool thread, used for needlepoint, is made through the same process but is heavier than crewel wool, and often comes in two, three, or four dividable strands.

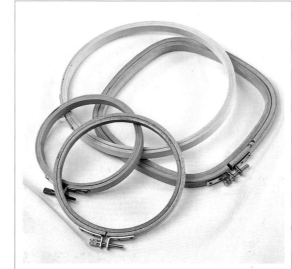

EMBROIDERY HOOPS

To have a smooth surface for embroidery, your fabric must be held taut. Embroidery hoops do just that; the fabric is sandwiched between two nestled rings that are screwed snugly together so that the fabric is tight, like a drum.

Hoops come in different shapes and sizes. They are round, oval, or square, and made of wood, plastic, or metal. A simple, round, unfinished wood hoop that you'll find at most craft stores will get you started. All of the patterns and projects in this book can easily be done using a round hoop, 6 inches (15.25 cm) in diameter. If crewelwork becomes your thing, you may want to invest in several different sizes of the smooth hardwood hoops, sold at needlecraft stores or online shops that carry tools for needlepoint, crewel, and cross-stitch.

In addition to hoops, adjustable wooden slat frames and uphol-stered wood pin frames can be used to hold embroidery fabric taut. Both of these frame types are square or rectangular, and very useful for large crewelwork projects.

THREAD CARD OR THREAD RING

If crewelwork becomes an obsession for you, you might want to make a thread card or find a wooden ring to keep your thread organized, as Jane Rainbow suggests in her book *Beginner's Guide to Crewel Embroidery* (Search Press, 1999). For the thread card, you'll need a piece of cardstock and a hole-punch. Punch a series of holes at least 2 inches (5 cm) apart and about 1/2 inch (1.25 cm) from one edge of the cardstock. Fold a handful of cut lengths of crewel wool thread in half, and thread this folded end into one of the holes, entering from the front of the card. A loop will form. Grasping the cut ends, slide them into the loop and pull until the loop is snug on the card. Write the corresponding name, color number, and brand name next to each loop. If you like, punch three holes along the opposite edge of the card and store it in a three-ring binder. As your collection grows, you can add cards to your binder. Another option for storing threads is to use a wooden ring, like the inside ring of an embroidery hoop. Loop the threads around the ring and sort by either color number or color.

NEEDLES

For crewel embroidery, you can use either a *crewel* needle or a *chenille* needle. Unlike tapestry needles, which are commonly used for needlepoint and cross-stitch, chenille and crewel needles have very sharp points. The crewel needle is longer, with a short eye. The chenille needle is shorter, with a long eye. When working on

tightly woven linen twill, I recommend that you use either a size 3, 4, 5, or 6 crewel needle or a size 20, 22, or 24 chenille needle (the bigger the number, the smaller the needle). Most of the crewelwork in this book was done using a size 24 chenille needle.

The right needle size depends on both your own comfort and the fabric you're using. For easier threading and for beginners, it might be better to begin with a larger needle (i.e., a size 20 chenille or a size 3 crewel). But given that the needle's key function is to guide the thread back and forth through the fabric, it is important to pick one that is neither too big nor too small. The correct size needle will make a temporary hole in the linen fabric for the thread to easily pass through. If your needle is too small, the thread will quickly wear out as it is dragged through the tight fabric on each pass. And if your needle is too large, it may create unnecessary work for you as you push it through the fabric each time, and it may distort the fabric so much that the temporary holes don't disappear after stitching. By the way, as hard as it is to imagine, too much embroidery can be . . . um, cruel. Not only do fingers wear out, but needles do, too. When the point of your needle starts to dull, pick a new one.

When your embroidery is finished, you may want to stitch it into something else like a pillow or an eyeglass case. For all of the projects in this book that needed additional stitching, I hand-stitched them using hand quilter's thread and a hand sewing needle called a *betweens* needle. You can use any good quality sewing thread and a *sharps,* or a

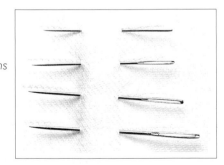

darner needle, as well. Betweens, sharps, and darners are the most common needles found in Grandma's sewing box. They vary in size and length, but all have fairly small eyes. Choose the needle that works best for you.

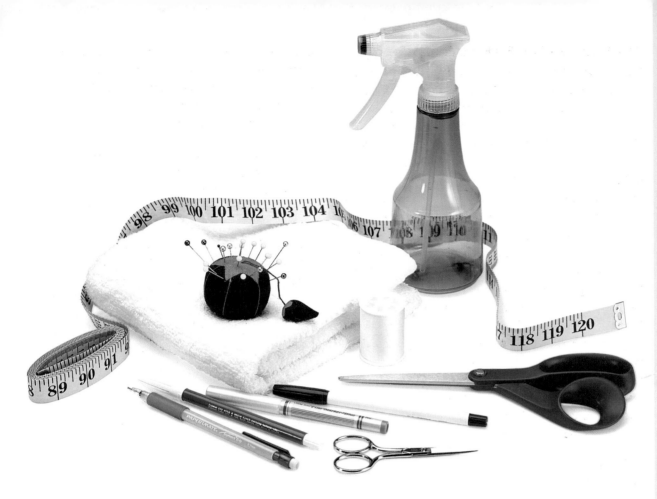

TOOLS

If you're a home sewer, you probably have most of these tools on hand.

SCISSORS

While one little pair of embroidery scissors will suffice for snipping your crewelwork threads, you will need a larger pair of fabric scissors capable of cutting your linen twill. In addition, it's nice to have a pair of pinking shears, with blades that are notched in a zigzag pattern. Cutting fabric with pinking shears helps to prevent the fabric from fraying while you work. Also, it's a fun way to quickly decorate the edge of a finished crewelwork for framing or making into a greeting card or book cover.

TRACING PAPER

To transfer the designs in this book (or designs of your own), you will need paper for tracing the design, a fabric pen or pencil, and a light source for tracing. It's best to get traditional translucent tracing paper, available at craft and art supply stores.

FABRIC PEN

Fabric pens are available at most fabric stores. The ink is usually blue or purple. I like both the water-erasable pens, which disappear with the slightest contact with water, and the air-vanishing pens that fade over time. Before you outline your design, test the fabric pen on a small corner of your fabric to be sure the ink really does disappear.

LIGHT TABLE OR SUNNY WINDOW

You'll need either a light table or a sunny window to backlight your design so that you can trace it onto the fabric.

ESSENTIAL SUPPLIES

You'll need the following basic household items for preparing your fabric before you trace a design, and for pressing your finished crewelwork: iron, ironing board, spray bottle, lightweight cotton cloth, and terrycloth towel. If your linen fabric is wrinkled, give it a quick press with a steam iron before transferring the design, or spray with clean water from your spray bottle and lightly press with a warm iron. When you are finished with your embroidery, you may choose to press it again. Always keep your iron set very low so that you don't toast your embroidery or the linen twill. To protect your crewelwork while pressing, turn the crewelwork face down on a white terrycloth towel and cover

it with a lightweight cotton cloth (such as a colorfast bandana, a kitchen towel, a handkerchief, or a press cloth). This helps to keep the design from getting flattened while pressing.

MEASURING TAPE, RULERS, AND CUTTING MATS

Every good embroiderer needs a classic dressmaker's measuring tape on hand for measuring fabrics and thread. A T-square ruler is also helpful for making sure your fabric cuts are always square. A plastic cutting mat with a measured grid drawn on one side, such as those used by quilters, is a perfect work surface for laying out small pieces of fabric, and it can withstand the impact of a pair of scissors, utility knife, or rotary blade.

STRAIGHT PINS

Have some basic straight pins handy for pinning various pieces and parts together if you plan to complete any of the projects in this book that require additional stitching.

DOUBLE-STICK FUSIBLE WEB

Double-stick fusible web is a brilliant invention. It is commonly sold in small packages, or by the yard from a 12-inch-wide (30.5 cm) roll. You'll find it near the interfacings in most fabric stores. The web is a gluey substance sandwiched between two pieces of waxed paper. After you have cut a piece to the size you need, peel the paper from one side. Place the sticky side down on the wrong side of your embroidery and give it a quick press with an iron on the side that still has paper on it. Peel off the remaining paper, leaving the glue on the backside of the embroidery. Now you have a sticky embroidery that can be ironed onto another paper or fabric surface, as I've done in the journal cover project (see page 66).

FABRIC GLUE OR WHITE GLUE

Basic white glue works well for tacking a finished design to a greeting card or a book cover. You can also buy glue specifically made for use with fabric. Remember, a little glue goes a long way. Use sparingly.

NEW CREWEL TECHNIQUES

The following are some basic techniques you'll need to know in order to get started with your first crewel project.

TRANSFERRING A DESIGN

The best (and age-old) way to transfer a design from paper to fabric is the sunny window trick. Here's how it works. If you're using a design from this book, place a piece of tracing paper over the design in the book and trace the design onto the tracing paper with a felt-tip pen. Now, take the tracing paper and tape it to a sunny window, making sure it is flat and secure on all sides. Next, tape your piece of linen twill (or whatever fabric you have chosen) squarely over the tracing paper. Using a fabric pen or pencil (even a regular No. 2 pencil works), trace the design again onto the fabric. Use short, light pencil strokes so as not to make the fabric shift over the tracing paper.

If you're lucky enough to have a professional light box (like photographers use), or if you have the do-it-yourself smarts to make your own, all the better. Follow the same instructions as above, but omit the sunny window part!

All of the designs in this book may be enlarged up to 200 percent. Use a copy machine to make your own custom size. For some of the larger designs, you may need to enlarge them in sections, and then tape the sections together to get the desired size.

HOOPING YOUR FABRIC

It's important to keep your fabric taut while you work so that there is no puckering in your crewelwork, and careful hooping does the trick. Hoops come in two parts: the inner hoop, which is a continuous piece of wood, and the outer hoop, which has a screw connector for tightening your fabric between the two pieces. Lay the inner hoop on a flat surface and center your fabric on top of it with your design facing up. Loosen the screw on the outer hoop so that it is loose enough to easily place over the fabric that is sitting on the inner hoop (fig. 1). Press the outer hoop down around

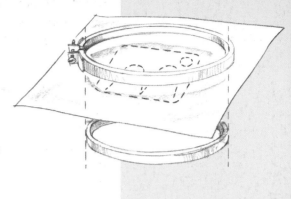

the inner hoop until the fabric is evenly caught between the two hoops. Adjust the fabric as necessary and tighten the screw on the outer hoop until the fabric is taut like a drum (fig. 2). The fabric will naturally loosen as you work, so occasionally you'll want to stop stitching and retighten your fabric in the hoop.

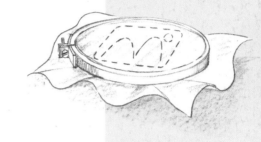

Although it's nice to be able to fit your design in the center of a hoop and not have to shift and rehoop as you work, this only works with small designs. If you get into bigger projects, you may need to move the hoop as you finish an area. It's okay to let your finished crewel areas get pinched in the hoop as you work on other areas. The wrinkles will all disappear in the end when you block your finished crewelwork. However, if you find you must leave your work for an extended time (days or weeks), undo the hoop and let the fabric relax until you have time to come back to it. It will thank you in the end.

THREADING THE NEEDLE

As you know, it's a crewel world out there, but don't let threading a needle be the deal-breaker. If you are new to this needle-'n-thread thing, take some time to learn it. You can do it. Eventually, you'll be able to thread a needle blindfolded. Really! So, follow these steps below. If you don't get it at first, try it again, and again. You are not allowed to give up at this step.

Take the thread in your dominant hand while holding the needle in your other hand. Make a 1-inch (2.5 cm) loop at one end of the thread. Lasso it around the needle and tug the thread away from the needle to make a crease (fig. 3). Slide the needle out and pinch the creased thread between your thumb and forefinger at the fold.

Figure 3

Guide the folded tip of the thread through the eye of the needle (fig. 4). If you're getting cross-eyed and can't seem to get it, keep your cool and know that there is a great little tool called a needle threader available at most fabric stores. But whatever you do, don't get frustrated. You *will* thread that needle and get crewelin'!

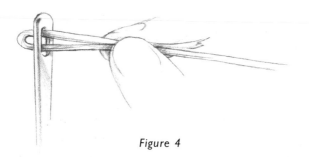

Figure 4

KNOTTING AND BEGINNING TO CREWEL

In crewelwork, it's traditional to have no knots in your finished work. But how do you start stitching if you can't tie a knot at the end of your thread? Here's how. After threading your needle, go ahead and make a knot at the end of the thread. Pick a spot on the front of your design that is about 2 inches (5 cm) from where you plan to begin stitching. At this spot, push your threaded needle through to the back. Yes, the knot will be on the front (fig. 5). Pull the thread taut and begin stitching your design. As you continue to sew, the thread that extends from the knot to where you started stitching

Figure 5

will eventually get caught up and covered on the underside of the fabric. When this happens, it's safe to carefully trim off the knot from the front of your work (fig. 6). The rest of the thread will naturally slip to the back, and if there's still a bit dangling, you can trim it again.

Figure 6

ENDING A THREAD

To end a thread, do not knot it. Remember, no knots in crewel (unless it's a French Knot). Instead, on the underside of your work, send the needle through several existing stitches without going through to the front (fig. 7). Do this back and forth two or three times. This will prevent the thread from pulling up on the front. After you've done this, trim any dangling threads. If you continue in this way, the underside of your crewelwork will stay smooth and without tatters, and will look nearly as nice as the front.

Figure 7

Once you've used up a thread, begin a new one in the same way you just ended the last one. Pull the newly threaded needle through several existing stitches on the underside of your work. Repeat this until the thread feels secure. Continue stitching. Note that linen twill fabric is much sturdier than crewel wool thread, so if your thread wears thin or starts to break, end it right away and pick up where you left off with a fresh one.

BLOCKING, STRETCHING, AND PRESSING

There are a couple of ways to finish your crewelwork so that it's ready to be turned into something else—a pillow, framed art, or other project. The best way is to use the traditional blocking technique. Simply put, you must stretch and square off your finished crewelwork on a wooden board, dampen it, and then let it dry. This works well and is very safe. The other way is slightly reckless, but it's quick, and works for small crewelworks where the design is no larger than 6 inches square (15 × 15 cm).

Here's the fast way: Lay your finished crewelwork face down on a terrycloth towel on top of an ironing board. Mist the crewelwork lightly with clean water from a spray bottle. Cover it with a thin piece of fabric, like a handkerchief. Using a medium warm iron, firmly press down on your embroidery, pulling the embroidered fabric at the corners as needed to make sure it stays in its original shape (fig. 8). You've got to work quickly so as not to scorch your work—just a couple of seconds of pressing at a time, just enough to press out the wrinkles. Repeat until your crewelwork is dry.

For traditional blocking, you'll need a clean board at least 3/4 inch (2 cm) thick that is larger in height and width than your finished crewelwork, a box of 1-inch (2.5 cm) round-headed, rustproof nails, and a hammer. Rinse your finished crewelwork completely in cold water. Lay the fabric face up and centered on the board. Starting in the center of the top edge of the fabric, tack a nail through the fabric into the board. Only about 1/4 inch (6 mm) of the nail needs to go

Figure 8

into the board. Smoothing the fabric with your hands and stretching it as necessary, tack a nail through the center of the bottom edge. Do the same in the center of the left and right edges.

Working from the centers to the corners, alternating top to bottom and then left to right, nail down the embroidery until all edges are nailed down. The spaces between each nail should be about 1 inch (2.5 cm). Be sure to keep the design square while you work. This may require stretching and pulling if your crewelwork lost its shape while you were embroidering. Set the board in a warm, airy place and let the crewelwork dry. If you're in a hurry, use a hairdryer to speed up the process. When your work is dry, remove the nails with a hammer or pliers. Your crewelwork is now blocked and ready to be framed or made into one of the projects featured in the last section of the book.

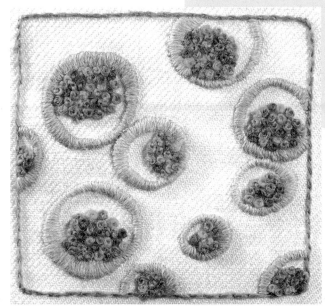

NEW CREWEL STITCHES

There are hundreds of crewel embroidery stitches. This section starts you out with just 16 of them, each of which is used at least once in the projects in this book. Know that this is just a beginning. There are many more stitches to be learned and many more still to be invented.

If you are familiar with embroidery, but new to crewel, you'll be happy to know that the stitches are virtually the same. The main difference between crewel embroidery and other kinds of embroidery is in the materials. Crewel is specifically done with two-ply worsted wool thread on linen fabric. Other types of embroidery use a myriad of materials from cottons to silks, including wool and linen.

If you've never embroidered before, I recommend practicing each stitch on a piece of scrap linen. When you are feeling confident, you can begin to use the stitches as shown in the designs in the second section of the book. Or go ahead and begin with the Framed Crewel Stitch Sampler (page 64), and learn each stitch as you complete your first New Crewel project.

The stitches in this section begin with the easy, breezy ones, then progress to more advanced stitches. New crewelers are urged to start at the beginning.

STRAIGHT STITCH

STRAIGHT STITCH

This is the simplest stitch in the whole crewel world. Send the threaded needle up from the back through to the front of your fabric at **A** (fig. 1). Then insert the needle down into the fabric front at **B** (fig. 2). Gently pull the threaded needle until the thread lies flat on the front of the fabric, and you're done (fig. 3). Easy.

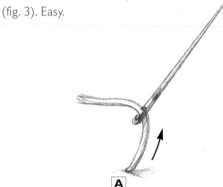

Figure 1

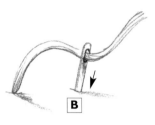

Figure 2

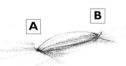

Figure 3

SEED STITCH

Seed stitch is made up of many very short Straight Stitches. Just as with Straight Stitch, send the threaded needle up from the back through the front of your fabric at **A**. Then insert the needle down into the fabric at **B** and pull through (fig. 4). Repeat (fig. 5) again and again, making the stitches very close to each other but not touching, in random directions, until you have created a surface that looks like many little "seeds" (fig. 6).

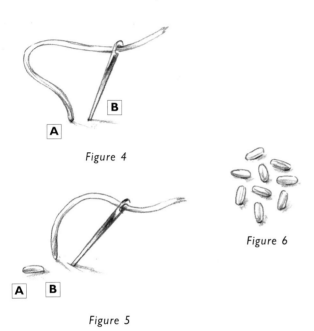

Figure 4

Figure 5

Figure 6

VARIATIONS

Make each Seed Stitch out of two or three stitches, one on top of other, so that each Seed Stitch stands up off the fabric.

Seed Stitch is also a good choice when you need the effect of shading in a design. Start on the edge that you want to be darker, making many Seed Stitches close together. Carefully thin them out until you have just a few on the side of your design that you want to look lighter. Voila!

BACK STITCH

Again, here's a stitch that's based on the Straight Stitch. Bring your threaded needle up at **A** and go down at **B** to make a Straight Stitch. Come up at **C** and go down at **A** again to make a second Straight Stitch (fig. 7). Come up again a stitch length ahead of **C**, then go down at **C**, and so on (fig. 8). It's a bit like window shopping—two steps forwards, one step back, two steps forward, one step back— as long as you keep going forward, you'll stay out of trouble. Note that Back Stitch can be done so that the stitches connect end-to-end, as in fig. 8, or with a small space between each stitch, as shown in the photograph at right.

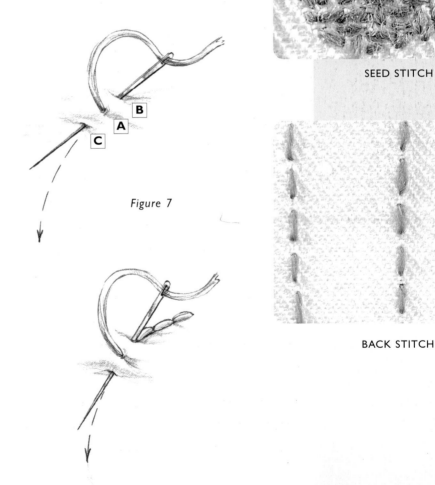

SEED STITCH

BACK STITCH

Figure 7

Figure 8

SPLIT STITCH

This is a versatile "drawing" stitch, great for outlining designs. First, make a single Straight Stitch. Bring the needle up through the middle of your Straight Stitch at **A**, then go down at **B** (fig. 9). Come up at **C**, again "splitting" the stitch, and go down at **D** (fig. 10), and so on. Hint: Keep all of your stitches the same size except when stitching around a tight curve. Accommodate the curve by making your stitches much smaller. This will keep the flow of the line very smooth. Just like driving a car—it's smart to slow down when turning a corner.

STEM STITCH/OUTLINE STITCH

Also known as Crewel Stitch or Stalk Stitch, this stitch is one of the most basic and common of all crewel stitches. It works well for outlining, especially for lines that curve. And it moves fast! The final effect is a line of stitches that looks like a rope. There are two ways to do this stitch. In the first, the true Stem Stitch, you hold the thread with your thumb below the line of stitching. To begin, bring your threaded needle up at **A**. While going down at **B** and holding the thread down with your thumb on the outside of the curve, come up at **C** half way between **A** and **B** (fig. 11). Let go of the thread under your thumb and pull the thread taut, then go back down at **D** and up again at **B**, holding thread down with your thumb (fig. 12). Repeat, keeping all of your stitches small and the exact same size (fig. 13 and fig. 14).

SPLIT STITCH

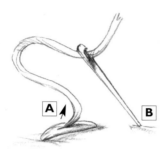

Figure 9

STEM STITCH

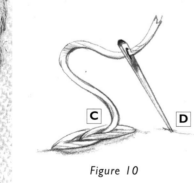

Figure 10

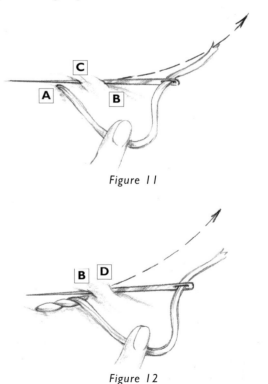

Figure 11

Figure 12

VARIATION

Stitch two lines of Split Stitch right next to each other to make an extra-thick line.

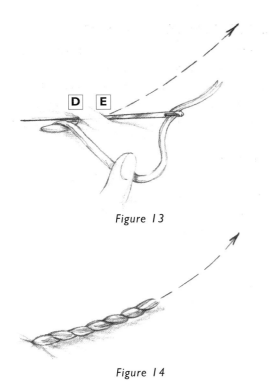

Figure 13

Figure 14

Outline Stitch, the second version of this stitch, is just like Stem Stitch, except that you hold the thread with your thumb above the line of stitching.

Keep the thread on the *outside* of the curve as you work, whether that is above or below the line of stitching. With either version, shorten your stitches when going around tight corners. This helps to make a cleaner, smoother line.

CHAIN STITCH

Like Split Stitch, Stem Stitch, and Back Stitch, Chain Stitch works well as an outline stitch. Use it when you need a bolder line in your designs. First, bring your threaded needle up at **A**. Holding the thread down with your thumb, create a loop as you insert the needle very close to, but not into, **A** (fig. 15). Bring the needle up through to the front of your fabric at **B** in the center of the loop (fig. 16). Pull the thread to shorten the loop so it spans from **A** to **B**. Again, while holding the thread down with your thumb, create a loop as you

insert the needle very close to, but not into, **B** (fig. 17). Pull the thread again until the length of the second loop spans from **B** to **C**, and bring the needle up at **C** (fig. 18). Insert the needle close to, but not into, **C** (fig. 19). Repeat until you have created a "chain" out of these loops (fig. 20). To end the chain, make a small stitch at the tip of the last loop.

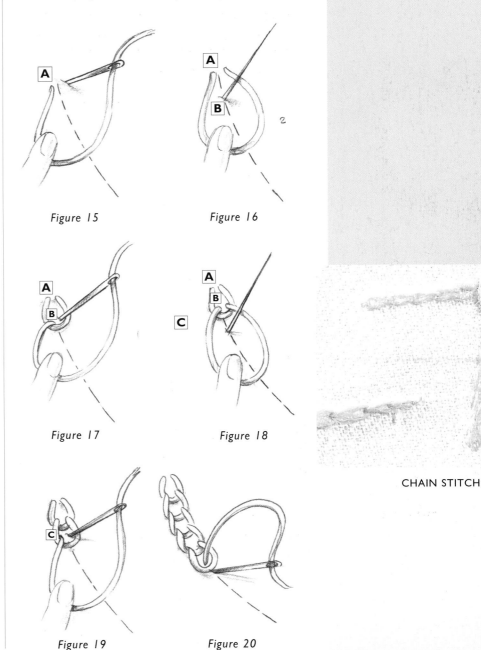

Figure 15

Figure 16

Figure 17

Figure 18

Figure 19

Figure 20

CHAIN STITCH

BLANKET STITCH

In crewelwork, Blanket Stitch is a simple but decorative linear stitch with unlimited variations. Begin by bringing your threaded needle up at **A**. Now, holding the thread down with your left thumb, send the needle down at **B** and come up at **C**. Keeping the yarn under the needle, pull the thread taut, forming a right angle (fig. 21). Send the needle down at **D** while holding the thread down with your left thumb coming up at **E** (fig. 22). Gently pull taut, forming another right angle, and repeat. Hint: For the best effect, try to keep the stitches the same length and the same distance apart, while maintaining an even tension.

SATIN STITCH

This is a classic embroidery stitch that looks easy, but requires practice to master. The version of Satin Stitch that I use is one I discovered in a book by Erica Wilson. It is a combination of the Straight Stitch and the Split Stitch. First, use Split Stitch to outline the area to be filled with Satin Stitch (fig. 23). Then, beginning at the widest part of the shape you are to fill, make Straight Stitches, one after the other, very close together, coming up at **A**, going down at **B**, coming up at **C**, going down at **D**, and so on (fig. 24). Hint: In order to get a soft, satiny finish, it is important to keep the tension of your thread the same throughout, not pulling too much or too little with each stitch (fig. 25).

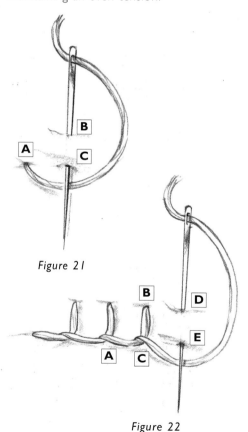

BLANKET STITCH

SATIN STITCH

Figure 21

Figure 22

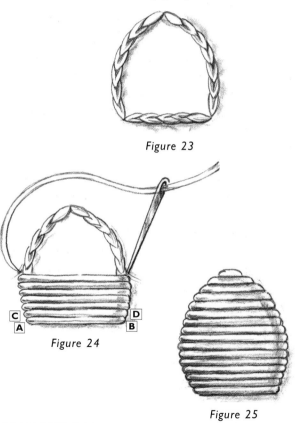

Figure 23

Figure 24

Figure 25

VARIATION

Make the length of the stitch from B to C longer than the stitch from D to E, and repeat over and over again to form a pattern.

VARIATION

Before doing the Straight Stitches on top of the outlined design, add Seed Stitches to the interior area of the outlined shape. This will make your Satin Stitch even puffier.

SATIN SHADING STITCH

Also known as the Long and Short Stitch or Soft Shading, this is the stitch that gives crewelwork its reputation of "painting with a needle and thread." Like Satin Stitch, this can be a tricky stitch to master, but it gives tremendous dimension to your designs when you get it right. It is similar to Satin Stitch in its application, but requires at least three close shades of the same color thread to achieve the illusion of a shadow.

Begin by outlining the design area with Split Stitch. Starting at the lighter side of the design, using the lightest shade of thread, make a row of Satin Stitches in alternating lengths covering about one third of the outlined area (fig. 26). Using the middle shade of thread, make another row of alternating-length Satin Stitches, this time bringing the needle up through the ends of the first row of Satin Stitches (fig. 27), covering the next third of the outlined area. Using the darkest shade of thread, make a final row of alternating-length Satin Stitches, again bringing the needle up through the ends of the second row of Satin Stitches, covering the rest of the outlined area (fig. 28).

Hints: When doing Satin Shading, always bring the needle UP through the last row of alternating length Satin Stitches, not down. Also, Satin Shading works best when you use long stitches, close together and sometimes overlapping. As you work, keep an eye on the way the colors blend. Add random stitches as necessary in order to create the illusion of shading.

Figure 26

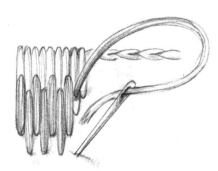

Figure 27

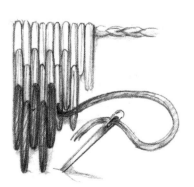

Figure 28

SATIN SHADING STITCH

OVERCAST STITCH

This is a cool stitch for making a puffy line. Traditionally, it is suggested that you first do a line of separated Straight Stitches for your foundation (also known as Running Stitch). Instead, I recommend using Split Stitch. So first, make a line out of Split Stitches (fig. 29). Then, make tiny, tiny Satin Stitches, one right after the other, completely covering the line of Split Stitch (fig. 30).

EYELET HOLE STITCH

I don't think this is specifically a crewel stitch, but I love it and find that it works well with crewel wool. Using Back Stitch, make a circle of stitching just inside the design line (fig. 31). Using a knitting needle, a sewing stiletto, or the tip of a scissors, carefully punch a hole in the fabric inside your stitches (fig. 32). If necessary, snip the fabric and trim close to the Back Stitch outline (fig. 33). Next, using Overcast Stitch, send your threaded needle down through the hole in the center and coming up at the edge of your design line, then down into the center and up again to form a stitch right next to the last one, covering the Back Stitch completely (fig. 34). Continue in this way, making sure to keep your stitches very close together until you have gone all the way around the hole (fig. 35).

OVERCAST STITCH

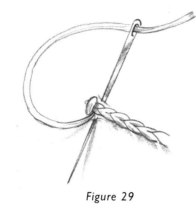

Figure 29

Figure 30

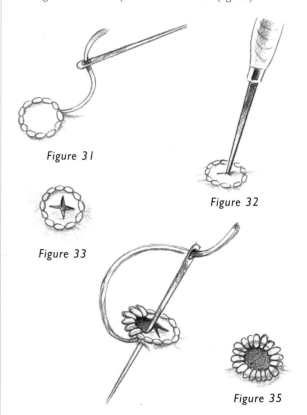

Figure 31

Figure 32

Figure 33

Figure 35

EYELET HOLE STITCH

VARIATION

Make your foundation line extra-thick with multiple lines of Split Stitch made right on top of each other. When you top that with Satin Stitch, you'll get a super-fat Overcast Stitch that will look really wormy on your fabric.

VARIATION

Make the width of the Overcast Stitch as thick or as thin as you like, or make it vary from thick to thin, creating a beautiful organic shape.

SPIDERWEB STITCH

Also known as Circular Spider's Web or Whipped Spider's Web. It looks tricky, but it's really not. Go ahead—give it a spin! Starting from the outer edge of your design and working toward the center, use Straight Stitch to make "spokes" that will form the structure of the web (fig. 36). Then slide the needle under spokes **A** and **B** near the center of the web (fig. 37). Pull your thread taut. Again slide the needle under spokes **B** and **C**. Pull your thread taut and toward the center of the web. Continue by sliding the needle under **C** and **D** and then under **D** and **E** (fig. 38), and so on, filling the web from the center out (fig. 39). Your web is finished when the spokes are no longer visible (fig. 40).

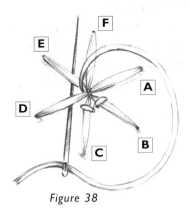

Figure 38

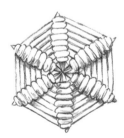

Figure 39

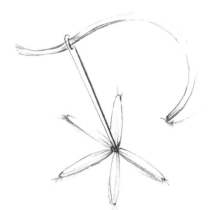

Figure 36

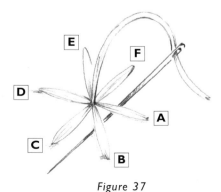

Figure 37

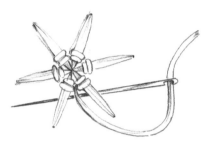

Figure 40

SPIDERWEB STITCH

VARIATION

Stop weaving the web halfway up the spokes so that the spokes are partially exposed.

29

FRENCH KNOT

Used as a single dot or in multiples to fill an area, the French Knot is fun! Bring your thread up to the front of your fabric at **A**. With the tip of the needle nearly touching the fabric at **A**, wrap the thread around the needle twice (fig. 41). Insert the needle very near where it came up at **A** (fig. 42). While pulling the thread nearly taut with your left hand, SLOWLY push the needle down through the fabric and pull taut on the underside. Presto! A knot will form on the surface (fig. 43).

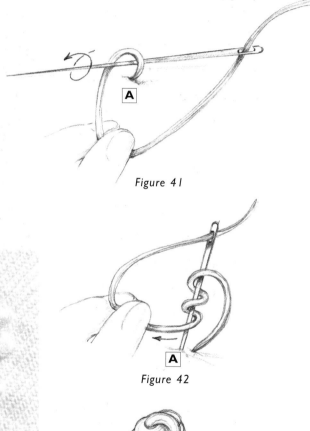

FRENCH KNOT

FRENCH KNOT STALK

FRENCH KNOT STALK

Sew sweet . . . this one's like candy on a stick! The French Knot Stalk, first introduced by Erica Wilson in the mid-1900s, is very similar to the standard French Knot. Send your thread up to the front of your fabric at **A**. With the tip of the needle nearly touching the fabric at **B**, wrap the thread around the needle twice (fig. 44). Insert the needle at **B** (fig. 45). While pulling the thread nearly taut with your left hand, slowly push the needle down through the fabric and pull taut on the underside. A knot will form on the surface, with a lovely "stalk" (fig. 46).

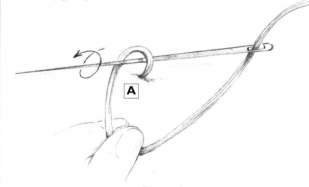

Figure 41

Figure 42

Figure 43

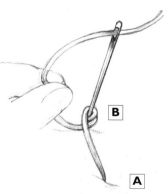

Figure 44

Figure 45

Figure 46

VARIATION

To make a smaller French Knot, wrap the thread around the needle only once. Similarly, wrap the thread three or four times to make it bigger.

30

CROSS STITCH FRENCH KNOT

First, make a Cross Stitch with two Straight Stitches (fig. 47). Then, bring the needle up where the two Straight Stitches intersect (fig. 48). Wrap the yarn around the needle twice and insert the needle into the fabric just on the other side of the crossed stitches (fig. 49). Pull the needle slowly through the fabric to form a French Knot at the center of the crossed stitches (fig. 50).

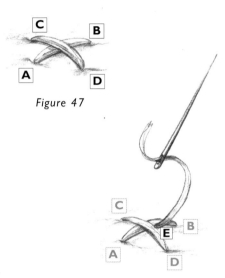

Figure 47

Figure 48

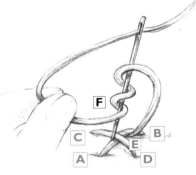

Figure 49

Figure 50

SQUARE FILLING STITCH

This stitch is perfect for adding texture and pattern to your crewel designs. Make several Straight Stitches running from opposite edges to form evenly spaced parallel lines (fig. 51). Repeat from the other two edges, creating a square grid (fig. 52). Using the same color or a contrasting color, make very small Straight Stitches at the intersections in the square grid until each intersecting pair of threads is tacked down (fig. 53).

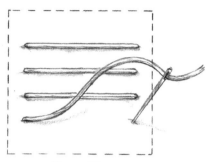

Figure 51

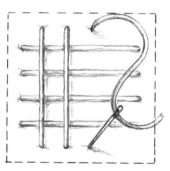

Figure 52

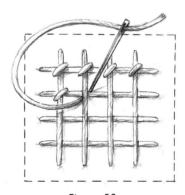

Figure 53

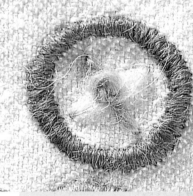

CROSS STITCH FRENCH KNOT

SQUARE FILLING STITCH

VARIATION

Add a French Knot in the center of each square in the grid.

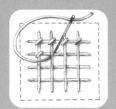

THE NEW CREWEL
GALLERY

The following collection of designs came directly from my sketch books. I carry a little black book with me wherever I go and am forever recording patterns, shapes, and textures that catch my eye. Back in my studio, I reinvent my findings and turn them into embroidery designs, paintings, or miniature sculptures. A few of them become Wool & Hoop crewel embroidery kits. The designs here were inspired by tiny desert flowers, patterns found on dilapidated buildings, and vintage thrift-store fabrics. But whatever the source, my embroidery designs get filtered through my palette—one that was born out of a small box of watercolors I carried through Italy as a young art student. I hope that you enjoy these 30 designs and are inspired to create your own.

Note: All of the designs in this chapter were embroidered using Appleton crewel wool thread with a size 24 chenille needle on Oyster White linen twill by Ulster Linen Co. Pattern and stitch diagrams for these designs begin on page 101. Each embroidery stitch is fully illustrated in the section on stitches, which begins on page 22. For instructions on enlarging and transferring the designs to fabric, and other notes on getting started, see the techniques section, which begins on page 19. For a myriad of ideas on what to do with your finished crewelwork, see the projects that start on page 63.

NEW CREWEL CIRCLE SAMPLER

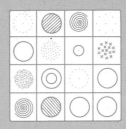

FABRIC

White linen twill, 12 inches square (30.5 x 30.5 cm)

THREAD

Crewel wool, 1 skein each pale yellow-green, white, and cream white*

STITCHES

Back Stitch, Blanket Stitch, Chain Stitch, Cross Stitch French Knot, Eyelet Hole Stitch, French Knot, French Knot Stalks, Overcast Stitch, Satin Stitch, Seed Stitch, Soft Shading, Spiderweb Stitch, Split Stitch, Square Filling Stitch, Stem Outline Stitch, Straight Stitch

FINISHING

Go to page 64 to see this design matted and framed.

CREWEL FACT

Samplers have been used for hundreds of years as a way to learn and display a set of stitches. It's traditional to stitch your name and the date on the lower edge of the design. After you've completed this one, find 16 more stitches in other embroidery books and make another sampler.

*The author used Appleton crewel wool in colors 331A, 991, and 992.

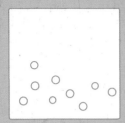

FABRIC

White linen twill, 12 inches square (30.5 × 30.5 cm)

THREAD

Crewel wool, 1 skein white*

STITCHES

Eyelet Hole Stitch, Split Stitch

FINISHING

Go to page 87 to see this design used on a lamp-shade.

CREWEL TIP

Use this design to embellish the edge of a curtain, table-cloth, skirt, pant leg, or sleeve. Make the holes big or small. Just remember that the hole you cut out will nearly double in size once it is stitched. Don't worry about making the hole perfect—the hand-made touch sets crewel-work apart from machine embroidery.

*The author used Appleton crewel wool in color 991.

FALLING SNOW

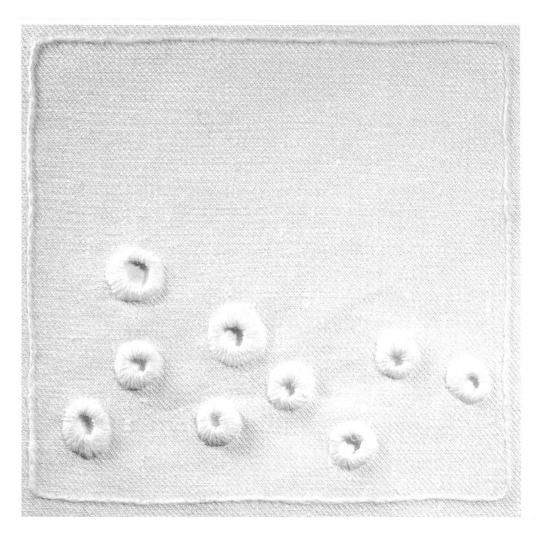

FISHING NET

FABRIC
White linen twill, 9 inches square (22.75 × 22.75 cm)

THREAD
Crewel wool, 1 skein each palest flesh, dark orange, and white*

STITCHES
Overcast Stitch, Split Stitch

FINISHING
Try matting and framing this design using the instructions for Cool Crewel Art (page 70), along with Snow Shoes (page 36), and Moon Rock (page 37).

CREWEL FACT
Steel needles with eyes were invented in England in the 17th century. Before that, embroiderers used needles made of bone, wood, or ivory, or iron needles that had no eyes but were threaded by a hook.

*The author used Appleton crewel wool in colors 701, 864, and 991.

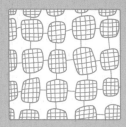

FABRIC
White linen twill, 9 inches square (22.75 x 22.75 cm)

THREAD
Crewel wool, I skein each palest flesh, dark orange, and white*

STITCHES
Split Stitch, Square Filling Stitch

FINISHING
Try matting and framing this design using the instructions for Cool Crewel Art (page 70), along with Fishing Net (page 35), and Moon Rock (page 37).

CREWEL REMINDER
Working in white thread on white linen can be dangerous for the accident-prone. Find or make a special bag for your crewelwork to keep it clean while in transit, or while it's sitting on the coffee table.

*The author used Appleton crewel wool in colors 701, 864, and 991.

SNOW SHOES

MOON ROCK

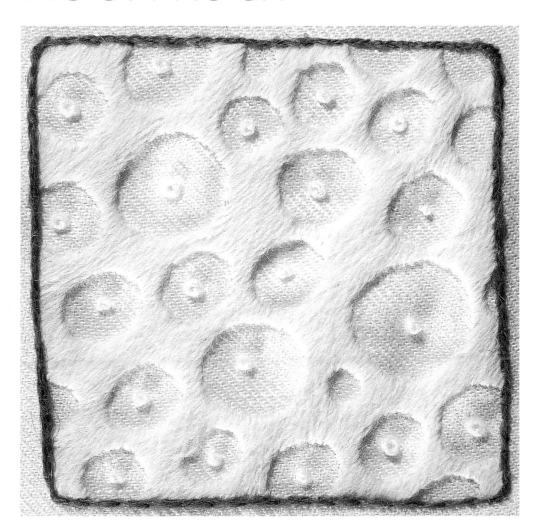

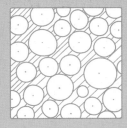

FABRIC
White linen twill, 9 inches square (22.75 x 22.75 cm)

THREAD
Crewel wool, I skein each palest flesh, dark orange, and white*

STITCHES
French Knot, Satin Stitch, Split Stitch

FINISHING
Try matting and framing this design using the instructions for Cool Crewel Art (page 70), along with Snow Shoes (page 36), and Fishing Net (page 35).

CREWEL REMINDER
To keep the fabric of your embroidery from fraying as you work, secure the edges with masking tape or trim with pinking shears.

*The author used Appleton crewel wool in colors 701, 864, and 991.

DINNER PARTY

FABRIC

White linen twill, 9 inches square (22.75 × 22.75 cm)

THREAD

Crewel wool, 1 skein each of bright orange, light blue-green, bright yellow-orange, sky blue, orange, dark orange, and light brown*

STITCHES

French Knot, Satin Stitch, Split Stitch

FINISHING

Go to page 90 to see this design used on an eyeglass case.

CREWEL REMINDER

When working the French Knots in this design, first do a run-through all in one color, placing a few in each blue ring. Then run through the second color, and so on, until you have completed knots in all four colors. Don't worry about being exact. Just be sure they are "clumped" together up against one side of the ring.

*The author used Appleton crewel wool in colors 442, 522, 556, 561, 862, 864, and 912.

38

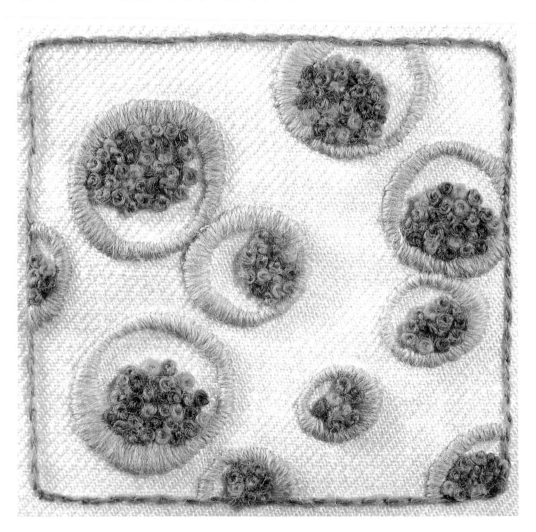

HIP SQUARES

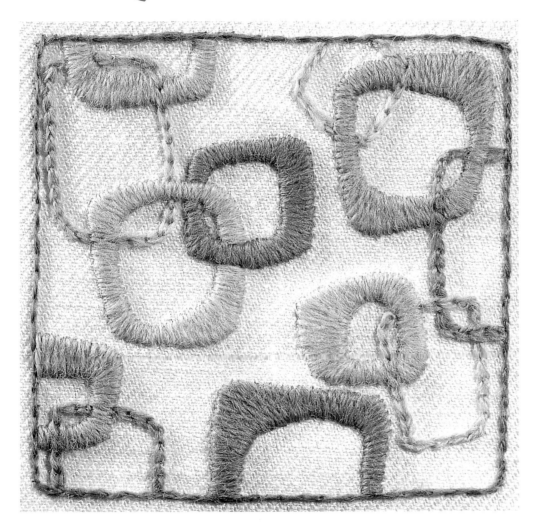

FABRIC

White linen twill, 9 inches square (22.75 x 22.75 cm)

THREAD

Crewel wool, 1 skein each of light blue-green, sky blue, light blue, and light brown*

STITCHES

Chain Stitch, Satin Stitch, Split Stitch

FINISHING

Go to page 70 to see this design matted and framed with Chainlink Pink (page 46) and Love Loops (page 47).

CREWEL REMINDER

Small, round hoops, 5 or 6 inches (12.75 or 15.25 cm) in diameter, are a nice size for most of the projects in this book. They fit well in the hand and can easily be thrown in a purse for the crewelgirl-on-the-go. For bigger projects, you may want to try a larger hoop or a slat frame—or just stick with a small hoop, and rehoop as you move around your design.

*The author used Appleton crewel wool in colors 522, 561, 742, and 912.

PUZZLE PIECE

FABRIC

White linen twill, 7 inches square (17.75 × 17.75 cm)

THREAD

Crewel wool, 1 skein each of light blue and chocolate brown*

STITCHES

French Knot, Satin Stitch

FINISHING

Go to page 75 to see this design in the Mason Jar Soft Tops project.

CREWEL TIP

When you use Satin Stitch to form rings (as opposed to straight lines), make your stitches closer together on the inside edge of the ring, and slightly farther apart on the outside edge. Also, it's helpful to always bring the needle up to the front of the fabric along the outside edge, and down to the back of the fabric along the inside edge.

*The author used Appleton crewel wool in colors 742 and 915.

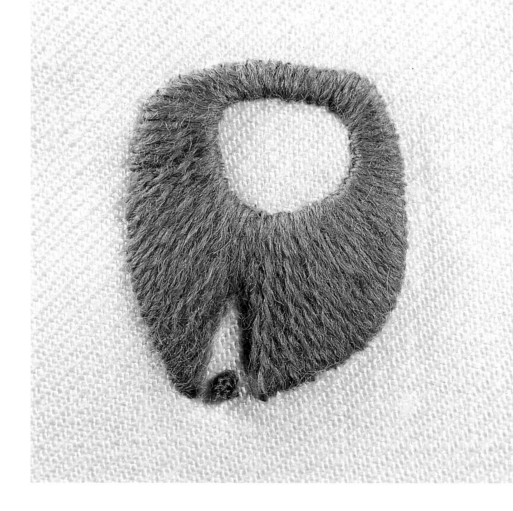

LITTLE CROWN

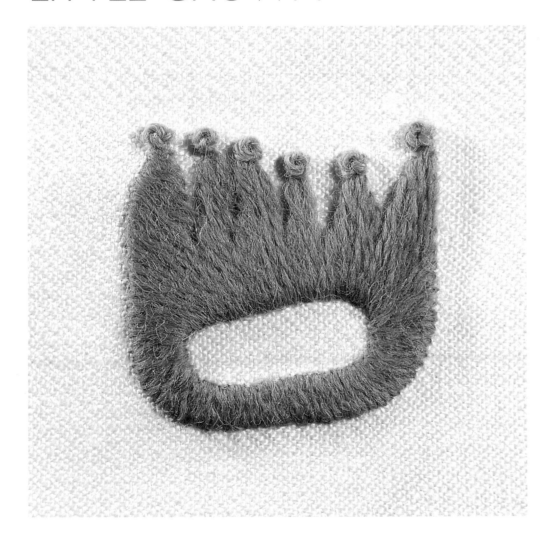

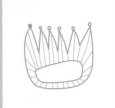

FABRIC

White linen twill, 7 inches square (17.75 x 17.75 cm)

THREAD

Crewel wool, 1 skein each of orange and medium pink*

STITCHES

French Knot, Satin Stitch

FINISHING

Go to page 75 to see this design in the Mason Jar Soft Tops project.

CREWEL TIP

Linen fabric, either plain or twill, is the most traditional ground material for crewel embroidery. It is known for its durability and nice sheen. Linen, which has been found in prehistoric dwellings, is made from the fiber of the flax plant. All of the designs in this book are worked on smooth white linen twill from Belgium.

*The author used Appleton crewel wool in colors 862 and 943.

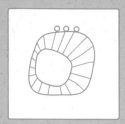

MAGIC RING

FABRIC
White linen twill, 7 inches
square (17.75 × 17.75 cm)

THREAD
Crewel wool, 1 skein each
of dark orange and medium
pink*

STITCHES
French Knot, Satin Stitch

FINISHING
Go to page 75 to see this
design in the Mason Jar Soft
Tops project.

CREWEL TIP
Create a whole new pat-
tern by repeating this
design over and over again,
either in rows, on a grid, or
randomly.

*The author used Appleton
crewel wool in colors 864
and 943.

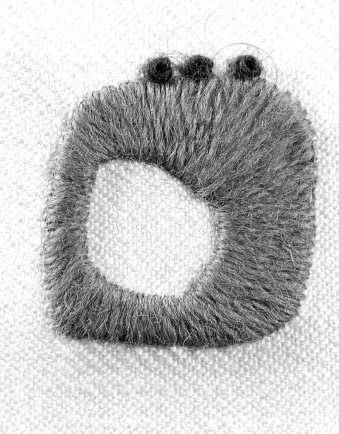

DAISY BLUES

FABRIC

White linen twill, 9 inches square (22.75 x 22.75 cm)

THREAD

Crewel wool, 1 skein each of sky blue, light blue, orange, and light brown*

STITCHES

French Knot, Satin Stitch, Split Stitch

FINISHING

Go to page 68 to see how you can use this design on a journal or scrapbook cover.

CREWEL REMINDER

Perfection in crewelwork is an ideal goal, but don't let it slow you down or bum you out. Just do it. Practice makes perfect.

*The author used Appleton crewel wool in colors 561, 742, 862, and 912.

TULIP TOPS

FABRIC

White linen twill, 9 inches square (22.75 x 22.75 cm)

THREAD

Crewel wool, 1 skein each of pale orange, light brown, medium pink, and pink. *

STITCHES

Satin Stitch, Split Stitch

FINISHING

Go to page 99 to see this design on a mesh zipper bag.

CREWEL FACT

The name "worsted," as in worsted wool, comes from the English town of Worstead, where this hard, smooth thread made from the wool of long-haired sheep was first perfected in the early 14th century.

*The author used Appleton crewel wool in colors 622, 912, 943, and 944.

BALLOON DROP

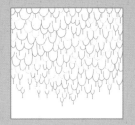

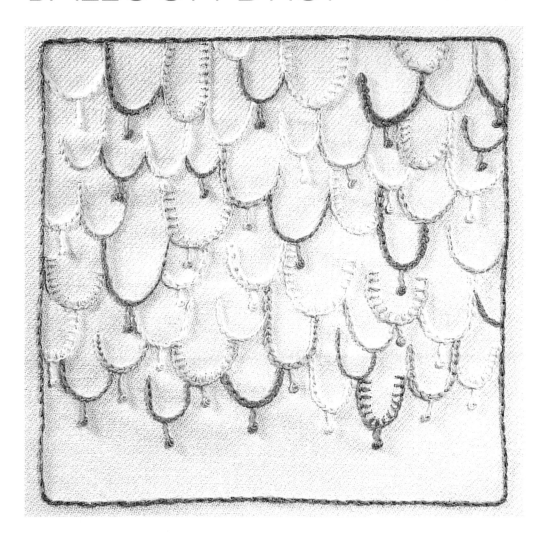

FABRIC

White linen twill, 12 inches square (30.5 x 30.5 cm)

THREAD

Crewel wool, 1 skein each of palest pink, light brown, light medium pink, medium pink, and pink*

STITCHES

Blanket Stitch, Chain Stitch, French Knot Stalks, Split Stitch

FINISHING

Go to page 78 to see how you can enlarge this design and make a pillow cover.

CREWEL REMINDER

All of the patterns in this book can be enlarged to up to 200 percent. Use a copy machine to make your own custom size.

*The author used Appleton crewel wool in colors 751, 912, 942, 943, and 944.

CHAINLINK PINK

FABRIC
White linen twill, 9 inches square (22.75 x 22.75 cm)

THREAD
Crewel wool, I skein each of light brown, light pink, and medium pink*

STITCHES
Satin Stitch, Split Stitch

FINISHING
Go to page 70 to see this design matted and framed, along with Hip Squares (page 39) and Love Loops (page 47).

CREWEL TIP
When making the long Satin Stitches that form the connections between the links in this design, use the same blending techniques outlined in the Satin Shading Stitch on page 27. Instead of making extralong stitches that go all the way across, make two or three shorter ones that overlap and get you to the other side.

*The author used Appleton crewel wool in colors 912, 941, and 943.

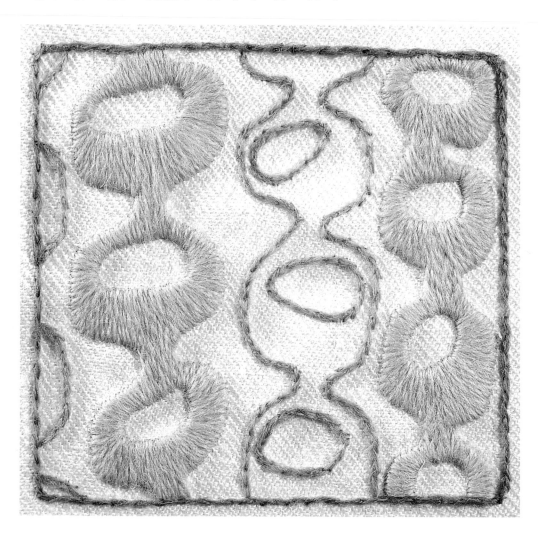

LOVE LOOPS

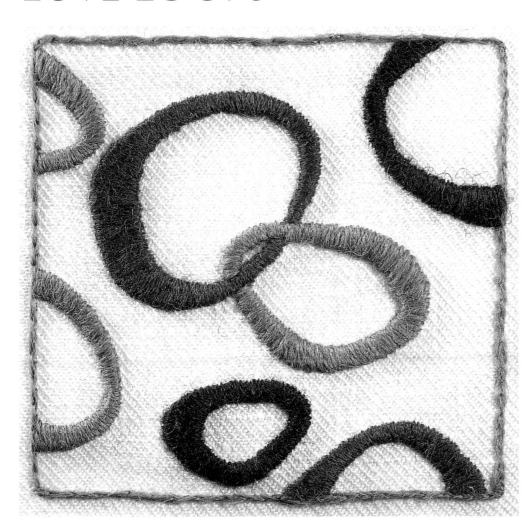

FABRIC

White linen twill, 9 inches square (22.75 x 22.75 cm)

THREAD

Crewel wool, 1 skein each of dark red, light brown, pink, and deep pink*

STITCHES

Satin Stitch, Split Stitch

FINISHING

Go to page 70 to see this design matted and framed, along with Hip Squares (page 39) and Chainlink Pink (page 46).

CREWEL FACT

Boys crewel, too. It's true. I know a male marathoner in Dallas who stitched a variation of this design on his lucky running shorts, and a man in Boston who crewels while watching football.

*The author used Appleton crewel wool in colors 503, 912, 944, and 946.

RUBY SHOOTS

FABRIC

White linen twill, 9 inches square (22.75 x 22.75 cm)

THREAD

Crewel wool, I skein each of dark red and light brown*

STITCHES

Split Stitch

FINISHING

Go to page 95 to see an embroidered wool skirt that was inspired by this design.

CREWEL FACT

The wool used in crewel embroidery comes from long-haired English sheep. Most American and Irish sheep have short, soft hairs.

*The author used Appleton crewel wool in colors 503 and 912.

SWAY DAYS

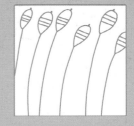

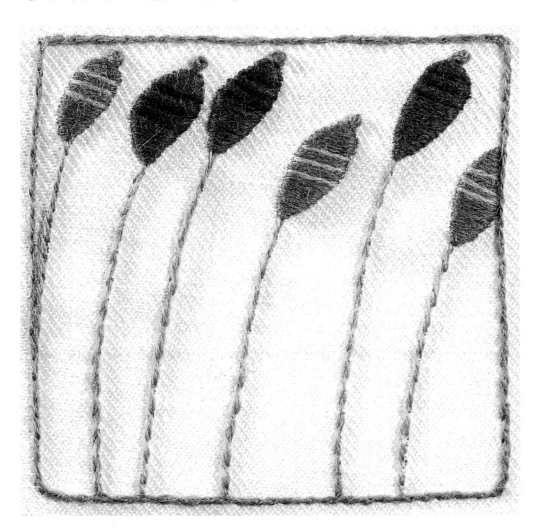

FABRIC

White linen twill, 9 inches square (22.75 x 22.75 cm)

THREAD

Crewel wool, 1 skein each of dark red, light brown, light medium pink, pink, periwinkle blue, and deep pink*

STITCHES

French Knot, Satin Stitch, Split Stitch, Stem Outline Stitch, Straight Stitch

FINISHING

Go to page 66 to see how you can turn this design into a greeting card.

CREWEL FACT

If threading your needle is driving you crazy, pick up a needle threader at your local fabric store. It will save your eyes and keep you in stitches.

*The author used Appleton crewel wool in colors 503, 912, 942, 944, 893, and 946.

SWEETHEART GARLAND

FABRIC

White linen twill, 9 inches square (22.75 x 22.75 cm)

THREAD

Crewel wool, 1 skein each of light autumn yellow, medium autumn yellow, palest yellow, light brown, and dark pink*

STITCHES

Soft Shading, Split Stitch

FINISHING

Go to page 68 to see how you can use this design as a journal cover.

CREWEL REMINDER

Even though a size 24 chenille needle is recommended for most of the projects in this book, you may feel more comfortable with a larger needle. The size of the needle gets bigger as the number get smaller. For example, a size 20 is a bigger needle than a size 24.

*The author used Appleton crewel wool in colors 471, 472, 841, 912, and 945.

SPRING FLING

FABRIC
White linen twill, 9 inches square (22.75 x 22.75 cm)

THREAD
Crewel wool, I skein each of light brown, pink, and deep pink*

STITCHES
Satin Stitch, Split Stitch, Straight Stitch

FINISHING
You'll find many ideas for using your finished embroidery in the projects.

CREWEL FACT
Nuns in medieval England were allowed to practice their embroidery, but only if it didn't get in the way of their daily devotions.

*The author used Appleton crewel wool in colors 912, 944, and 946.

FABRIC

White linen twill, 9 inches square (22.75 × 22.75 cm)

THREAD

Crewel wool, 1 skein each of dark red, light periwinkle blue, medium periwinkle blue, periwinkle blue, light brown, pink, and deep pink*

STITCHES

Soft Shading, Split Stitch

FINISHING

This design would look lovely on a pillow (see page 78).

CREWEL FACT

Some favorite popular songs, for which 'crewel' might be substituted for another word, include "Don't Be Crewel," by Elvis Presley; "Crewel To Be Kind," by Nick Lowe; "High On Crewel," by Neko Case; and "Sew Crewel," by U2.

*The author used Appleton crewel wool in colors 503, 891, 892, 893, 912, 944, and 946.

BLUE AGAVE

SCARLET SPARKS

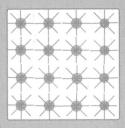

FABRIC

White linen twill, 9 inches square (22.75 x 22.75 cm)

THREAD

Crewel wool, I skein each of dark red, light brown, and pink*

STITCHES

Spiderweb Stitch, Split Stitch

FINISHING

Go to page 97 to see an embroidered scarf that was inspired by this design.

CREWEL TIP

This pattern uses the Spiderweb Stitch. In the illustration, each web is only partially completed, so the spokes really stick out. Feel free to mix it up a bit— make some of the Spiderwebs complete, so the spokes are covered, and keep some of them only partially done.

*The author used Appleton crewel wool in colors 503, 912, and 944.

FABRIC

White linen twill, 9 inches square (22.75 x 22.75 cm)

THREAD

Crewel wool, 1 skein each of periwinkle blue, light brown, and deep pink*

STITCHES

Blanket Stitch, French Knot, Split Stitch

FINISHING

Go to page 93 to see this design embroidered on a chef's apron.

CREWEL IDEAS

Do crewelwork embellishments on a fleece blanket or your favorite wool sweater; make potholders and a chef's hat to go with the apron on page 93; make a special baby quilt made up of lots of crewelwork squares.

*The author used Appleton crewel wool in colors 893, 912, and 946.

RASPBERRY TREATS

COOL STARBURSTS

FABRIC
White linen twill, 9 inches square (22.75 x 22.75 cm)

THREAD
Crewel wool, 1 skein each of palest periwinkle blue, medium blue, periwinkle blue, and light brown*

STITCHES
Spiderweb Stitch, Split Stitch, Straight Stitch

FINISHING
Go to page 72 to see this design used as sachet or tree ornament, and go to page 85 to see a pair of embroidered blue jeans.

CREWEL IDEA
How about embellishing your blue jean jacket, skirt, vest, or a denim bag? True crewel blue!

*The author used Appleton crewel wool in colors 461, 744, 893, and 912.

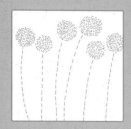

FABRIC

White linen twill, 9 inches square (22.75 x 22.75 cm)

THREAD

Crewel wool, 1 skein each of lavender, olive brown, palest periwinkle blue, periwinkle blue, and light brown *

STITCHES

Back Stitch, Seed Stitch, Split Stitch

FINISHING

Go to page 82 to see this design on a lavender-filled eye pillow.

CREWEL TIP

Here's a crewel rule of thumb: Short threads for short stitches, long threads for long stitches. As you work, different stitches can wear out your worsted wool thread at different rates. When you're working with a small stitch, such as Seed Stitch, use shorter pieces of thread so that they don't wear out too quickly (about 8 to 10 inches, or 20 to 25 cm). When your stitches are long, such as Satin Stitch, use longer pieces of thread (12 to 14 inches, or 30.5 to 35.5 cm).

*The author used Appleton crewel wool in colors 102, 312, 461, 893, and 912.

WILD BUNCH

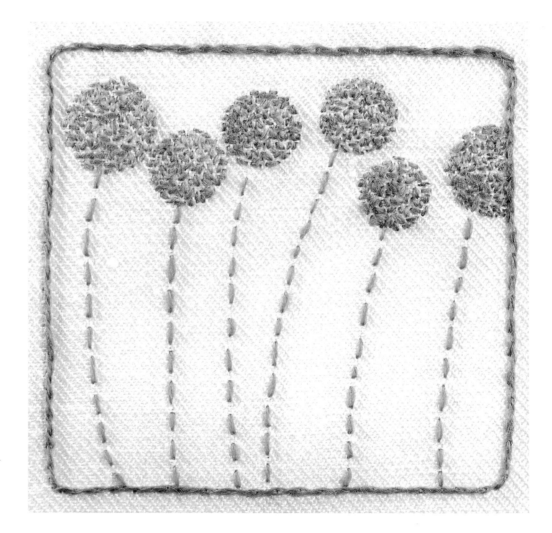

BIRTHDAY WISH

FABRIC
White linen twill, 9 inches square (22.75 x 22.75 cm)

THREAD
Crewel wool, 1 skein each of light brown, olive brown, pink, and deep pink

STITCHES
French Knot, Satin Stitch, Split Stitch, Straight Stitch

FINISHING
Go to page 66 to see how you can turn this design into a greeting card.

CREWEL REMINDER
When working in Satin Stitch, always keep your threads going in the same direction. For example, if you are filling a shape and working from the left to the right, continue from the left to the right over and over again until you are finished.

*The author used Appleton crewel wool in colors 912, 312, 944, and 946.

FABRIC

White linen twill, 9 inches square (22.75 x 22.75 cm)

THREAD

Crewel wool, 1 skein each of palest spring green, palest sage green, and light brown*

STITCHES

Satin Stitch, Split Stitch

FINISHING

Go to page 69 to see this design used as a journal cover.

CREWEL REMINDER

In designs like this one, where branches appear to overlap, remember that it's just an illusion. Be sure to end your Satin Stitch when it appears that you should be going under a branch, and then pick it up again on the other side of the branch. Otherwise, you'll end up with big lumps where the branches intersect.

*The author used Appleton crewel wool in colors 251, 541, and 912.

PEACE TREE

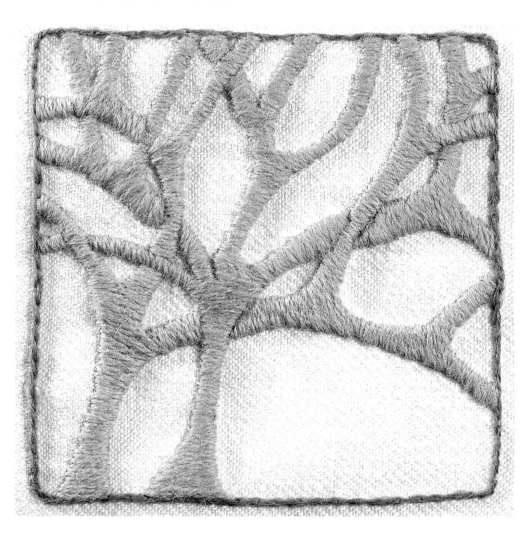

QUEEN'S LACE

FABRIC

White linen twill, 12 inches square (30.5 x 30.5 cm)

THREAD

Crewel wool, 1 skein each of light spring green, medium spring green, spring green, light sage green, palest flesh, light brown, and white*

STITCHES

Chain Stitch, French Knot, Split Stitch, Stem Outline Stitch

FINISHING

Go to page 78 to see how you can enlarge this design and turn it into a pillow cover.

CREWEL REMINDER

It's good practice to keep the underside of your crewelwork from getting too messy. Keep knots to a minimum, and try not to run a thread across a large open section on the back. It will eventually show through the white fabric to the front.

*The author used Appleton crewel wool in colors 251A, 252, 253, 543, 701, 912, and 991.

FABRIC

White linen twill, 9 inches square (22.75 x 22.75 cm)

THREAD

Crewel wool, 1 skein each of light blue, sky blue, dark orange, orange, bright orange, and pale orange*

STITCHES

Overcast Stitch, Cross Stitch French Knot, Split Stitch

FINISHING

Many ideas for using your finished embroidery appear starting on page 63.

CREWEL FACT

Another name for an embroidery hoop is *tambour*, a French word meaning drum. Fabric tautly stretched in the hoop, looks like a drum—or like a tambourine.

*The author used Appleton crewel wool in colors 742, 561, 864, 862, 442, and 622.

SWEET BUTTONS

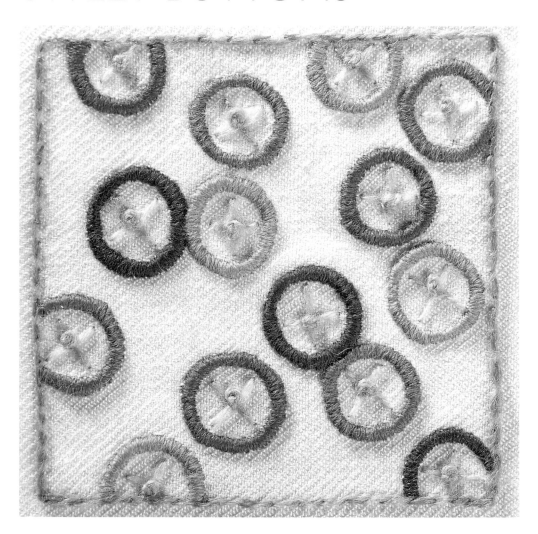

BABY GREENS

FABRIC
White linen twill, 9 inches square (22.75 x 22.75 cm)

THREAD
Crewel wool, I skein each of palest spring green, medium spring green, light autumn yellow, medium autumn yellow, palest sage green, palest yellow, and light brown*

STITCHES
Satin Stitch, Split Stitch

FINISHING
Go to page 68 to see how you can use this design as a journal cover.

CREWEL REMINDER
Crewelwork is the perfect companion for that long drive to grandma's house. Pack a little kit for your trip—but only if you're in the passenger's seat, of course. Please, don't crewel and drive.

*The author used Appleton crewel wool in colors 251, 252, 471, 472, 541, 841, and 912.

61

STAR FISH

FABRIC
White linen twill, 12 inches square (30.5 × 30.5 cm)

THREAD
Crewel wool, 1 skein each of palest yellow and light autumn yellow*

STITCHES
Chain Stitch, Satin Stitch, Split Stitch

FINISHING
How about stitching this design onto a beach tote bag?

CREWEL REMINDER
I sew, therefore I am.

*The author used Appleton crewel wool in colors 841 and 471.

THE NEW CREWEL
PROJECTS

FRAMED STITCH
SAMPLER

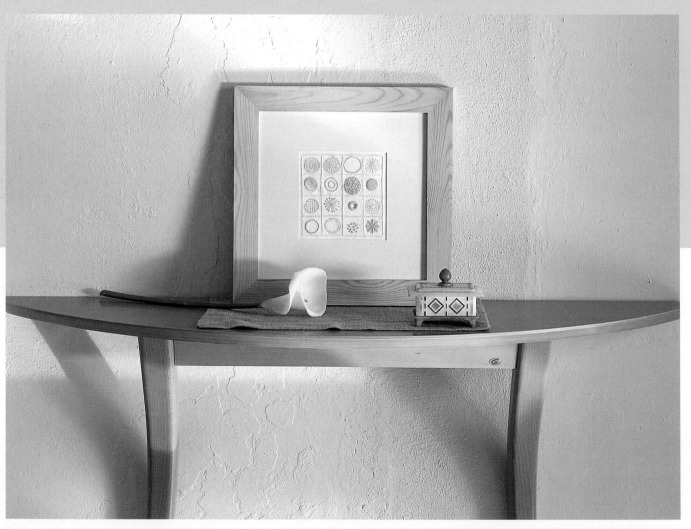

This lovely sampler includes all of the stitches illustrated in this book on one piece of fabric. Have your sampler matted and framed professionally, or do it yourself, following our instructions. Hang your finished sampler on the wall and refer to these basic crewel embroidery stitches as you work on the rest of the projects in the book.

WHAT YOU NEED

For the Sampler

White linen twill, 12 inches square (30.5 x 30.5 cm)

Hoop, 9 inches (22.75 cm) in diameter

Crewel wool thread, 1 skein each of white, cream white, and pale yellow-green

Chenille needle, size 24, or comparable crewel needle of choice

Tracing paper

Fabric pen or pencil

Scissors

INSTRUCTIONS

 1

Using the tracing paper and the fabric pen or pencil, transfer the New Crewel Circle Sampler pattern squarely onto the center of the linen fabric (see page 19).

2

Hoop the fabric, centering the design in the hoop (see page 19).

3

Begin by embroidering the outline of the grid using the stitches indicated in the New Crewel Circle Sampler diagram.

4

Proceed by embroidering each circle in each square, using the stitches indicated in the diagram.

5

Trim approximately 1 inch (2.5 cm) from all sides.

6

Block the finished sampler (see page 21).

WHAT YOU NEED

For the Mat and Frame

White archival mat board to match linen twill, 14 inches square (35.5 x 35.5 cm)

Archival foam-core board, 14 inches square (35.5 x 35.5 cm)

Contemporary wood frame with glass or clear plastic sheeting, 14 inches square (35.5 x 35.5 cm)

Pencil

Ruler

Mat cutter

Tape, archival or acid-free (available at art supply stores)

INSTRUCTIONS

1

Using the pencil and the ruler, mark a 6$\frac{1}{2}$-inch-square (16.5 x 16.5 cm) opening in the center of the white archival mat board.

2

Cut out the opening using your mat cutter.

3

Mount the sampler on the mat board by centering the embroidery in the mat opening, facing out, and taping the wrong side of the embroidery to the inside of the mat board (fig. 1).

4

Place the foam-core board behind the sampler, and attach with a hinge made of tape (fig. 1).

5

Insert the matted embroidery into the frame.

The author used Appleton crewel wool in colors 991, 992, and 331A.

PATTERN

New Crewel Circle Sampler (see page 101)

STITCHES

Straight Stitch, Satin Stitch, Back Stitch, Spiderweb Stitch, Chain Stitch, French Knot, Eyelet Hole Stitch, Cross Stitch French Knot, Seed Stitch, Split Stitch, French Knot Stalk, Blanket Stitch, Stem Stitch (Outline Stitch variation), Satin Shading Stitch, Square Filling Stitch, and Overcast Stitch.

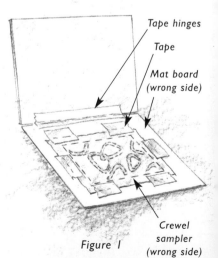

Tape hinges

Tape

Mat board (wrong side)

Crewel sampler (wrong side)

Figure 1

GREETING
CARD

Trim, fringe, and mount your crewel embroidery to the front
of a greeting card. Write a sweet (or crewel) note inside,
and give the card to a friend.

WHAT YOU NEED

White linen twill, 9 inches square (23 × 23 cm)

Hoop, 6 inches (15.25 cm) in diameter

Crewel wool thread, 1 skein each light brown, olive brown, pink, and deep pink

Chenille needle, size 24, or comparable crewel needle of choice

Double-stick fusible web, 3 inches square (7.5 × 7.5 cm)

Blank greeting card, 5 inches square (12.75 × 12.75 cm), and matching envelope

Tracing paper

Fabric pen or pencil

Scissors

Pinking shears

INSTRUCTIONS

Using the tracing paper and the fabric pen or pencil, transfer the Birthday Wish pattern squarely onto the center of the fabric (see page 19).

2

Hoop the fabric, centering the design in the hoop (see page 19).

3

Begin by embroidering the outline of the design using Split Stitch.

4

Proceed by embroidering the design inside the square, using the stitches and colors indicated in the Birthday Wish diagram.

5

Block the finished embroidery (see page 21).

6

Using your pinking shears, trim all sides of the fabric, leaving about 1/4 inch (.5 cm) outside of the Split Stitch outline.

7

Lay your embroidery face down on a terrycloth towel on the ironing board. Peel the loose paper from one side of the fusible web, and place the sticky side squarely on the underside of your embroidery. Cover with a cloth and press firmly with a warm iron.

8

Place the greeting card, front side up, on a hard surface that is covered with a cloth for protection, such as an ironing board. Slowly peel off the remaining sheet of paper from the fusible web on the back of your embroidery. Center your embroidery on the card front. Flip the card over so the embroidery is face down, and place a thin cloth (such as a bandana) over the card. Press evenly with a warm iron for about five to 10 seconds, or until the embroidery is adhered to the card. Work quickly so that you do not scorch your embroidery or the card.

VARIATION

After blocking your finished embroidery, trim all sides of the fabric with fabric scissors, leaving about 1/4 inch (.5 cm) outside of the Split Stitch outline. Then, gently pull the free threads, one at a time, until you have a nice fray on all four sides. Continue with #7 above to create a greeting card.

The author used Appleton crewel wool in colors 912, 312, 944, and 946.

PATTERN

Birthday Wish (see page 108)

STITCHES

Split Stitch, Straight Stitch, Satin Stitch, French Knot

JOURNAL OR SCRAPBOOK
COVER

Embellish a journal or scrapbook with crewel embroidery that is trimmed, fringed, and glued to the front cover. You can also look for a blank book made with a pre-cut opening for inserting a picture. If you're a book artist and know how to make your own book, even better!

WHAT YOU NEED

White linen twill, 9 inches square (23 × 23 cm)

Hoop, 6 inches (15.25 cm) in diameter

Crewel wool thread, 1 skein each of light brown, palest sage green, and palest spring green

Chenille needle, size 24, or comparable crewel needle of choice

Any handmade or purchased journal at least 4 inches square (10 × 10 cm)

Tracing paper

Fabric pen or pencil

Scissors

Pinking shears

Fabric glue

INSTRUCTIONS

1

Using the tracing paper and the fabric pen or pencil, transfer the Peace Tree pattern squarely onto the center of the fabric (see page 19).

2

Hoop the fabric, centering the design in the hoop (see page 19).

3

Begin stitching by embroidering the outline of the design, using Split Stitch.

4

Proceed by embroidering the design inside the square, using Satin Stitch as indicated in the Peace Tree diagram.

5

Block finished embroidery (see page 21).

6

Using your pinking shears, trim all sides of the embroidery to within 1/4 inch (.5 cm) of the Split Stitch outline.

7

Lay your embroidery face down and apply a very thin layer of fabric glue to the back. Carefully center and smooth your embroidery onto the front of the journal. Wait for it to dry. Start recording your crewel thoughts!

VARIATIONS

After transferring the design to the fabric, use your fabric pen to write a simple phrase like "crewel thoughts" below the transferred design. Stitch the words, using Split Stitch, with a thread color of your choice.

After blocking your finished embroidery, trim all sides of the fabric with fabric scissors, leaving about 1/4 inch (.5 cm) outside of the Split Stitch outline. Then, gently pull the free threads, one at a time, until you have a nice fray on all four sides. Continue with #7 above to finish your journal cover.

The author used Appleton crewel wool in colors 912, 541, and 251.

PATTERN

Peace Tree (see page 108)

STITCHES

Split Stitch, Satin Stitch, French Knot

69

COOL CREWEL ART

Three crewel embroideries in contemporary frames make a modern, eye-catching grouping on the wall. Have the pieces matted and framed professionally, or try it yourself if you have a mat cutter.

WHAT YOU NEED

for the Embroideries

3 pieces of white linen twill, each 9 inches square (23 x 23 cm)

Hoop, 6 inches (15.25 cm) in diameter

Crewel wool thread in the following colors:

Hip Squares: 1 skein each of light blue-green, sky blue, light blue, light brown

Chainlink Pink: 1 skein each of light brown, light pink, medium pink

Love Loops: 1 skein each of dark red, light brown, pink, deep pink

Chenille needle, size 24, or comparable crewel needle of choice

Tracing paper

Fabric pen or pencil

Scissors

INSTRUCTIONS

Using the tracing paper and fabric pen or pencil, transfer one design onto the center of each piece of linen twill fabric (see page 19).

2

Hoop one of the pieces of fabric, centering the design in the hoop (see page 19).

3

Embroider the outline of the design using Split Stitch.

4

Embroider the design inside the Split Stitch outline, using colors and stitches as indicated in the diagram for the design.

5

Repeat for the two other designs.

6

Block the finished embroideries (see page 21).

7

Trim approximately 1 inch (2.5 cm) from all sides, so that your finished pieces are now approximately 7 inches square (17.75 x 17.75 cm).

WHAT YOU NEED

for the Mats and Frames

3 pieces of white archival mat board to match linen fabric, each 12 inches square (30.5 x 30.5 cm)

3 pieces of archival foam-core board, each 12 inches square (30.5 x 30.5 cm)

Mat cutter

Tape, archival or acid-free

3 contemporary wood frames with glass or clear plastic sheeting, each 12 inches square (30.5 x 30.5 cm). Note: Many scrapbook stores offer frames in this size.

INSTRUCTIONS

Bevel-cut a 3 1/2-inch-square (9 x 9 cm) opening in the center of each sheet of white archival mat board.

2

Mount one embroidery onto each mat board and back each with archival foam core board (see instructions for matting and framing the Framed Stitch Sampler, page 65).

3

Place one assembled mat with embroidery in each frame. Now hang your first pieces of Cool Crewel Art!

VARIATIONS

Choose from the many other designs in this book to embroider and frame as art.

Using a larger frame and larger mat board, cut two, three, or four openings in the mat board and frame several embroideries in one frame—three in a row, or two across, two down—however you like!

For Hip Squares, the author used Appleton crewel wool in colors 522, 561, 742, and 912.

For Chainlink Pink, the author used Appleton crewel wool in colors 912, 941, and 943.

For Love Loops, the author used Appleton crewel wool in colors 503, 912, 944, and 946.

PATTERNS

Hip Squares (see page 102)

Chainlink Pink (see page 104)

Love Loops (see page 104)

STITCHES

Split Stitch, Satin Stitch, Chain Stitch

SCENTED SACHET OR TREE
ORNAMENT

Turn your crewel embroidery into a sachet filled with dried flowers to hang
in a window or on a tree, or to toss in your lingerie drawer.

WHAT YOU NEED

White linen twill, 9 inches square (23 × 23 cm)

Hoop, 6 inches (15.25 cm) in diameter

Crewel wool thread, 1 skein each of light brown, periwinkle blue, medium blue, and palest periwinkle blue

Chenille needle, size 24, or comparable crewel needle of choice

White silk or cotton organdy (or another lightweight, natural fabric), 5 inches square (12.75 × 12.75 cm)

Satin ribbon, or any ribbon or string of your choosing, 6 inches (15.25 cm) or desired length

Dried lavender or any other fragrant dried flowers or potpourri

Tracing paper

Fabric pen or pencil

Scissors

Sewing thread to match fabric

Hand sewing needle

Straight pins

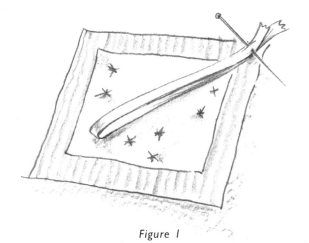

Figure 1

INSTRUCTIONS

1

Using the tracing paper and the fabric pen or pencil, transfer the Cool Starbursts pattern onto the center of the white linen twill fabric (see page 19).

2

Hoop the fabric, centering the design in the hoop (see page 19).

3

Embroider the outline of the design using Split Stitch.

4

Embroider the rest of design as indicated in the Cool Starbursts diagram.

5

Block the finished crewelwork (see page 21).

6

Trim 2 inches (5 cm) from each side of your embroidery, leaving a fabric border of about 1 inch (2.5 cm) on all sides.

7

Fold the ribbon in half so the two raw ends meet.

8

Lay the folded ribbon diagonally across the front of your crewelwork. Pin the raw edges of the folded ribbon to the outer edge of the crewelwork at the corner (fig. 1).

9

Pin the folded end of the ribbon to the front of the crewelwork to hold the ribbon in place.

10

With right sides together, pin the crewelwork to the square of silk or organdy fabric on all sides.

PATTERN

Cool Starbursts (see page 108)

STITCHES

Split Stitch,
Straight Stitch,
Spiderweb Stitch

11

With the sewing thread and hand sewing needle, stitch the two pieces together using Back Stitch, following the outside edge of the embroidered design and leaving a 2-inch (5 cm) opening in the center of one side for turning. Remove the pins.

12

Trim the seam allowances to ⅜ inch (1 cm). Trim corners close to, but not through, your stitching.

13

Turn the sachet right side out through the opening. Using the end of a blunt scissors, knitting needle, or chopstick, gently push out the corners. Be careful not to push too hard, or you'll poke a hole in your work.

14

Fill the sachet with dried flowers or potpourri.

15

Fold in the remaining seam allowance at the opening, pin, and stitch closed. Remove the pin that is securing the ribbon, and hang your sachet or toss in a drawer.

VARIATION

Using a heavier fabric than organdy for the backing—perhaps something colored or patterned—follow the same steps, but fill with polyester stuffing for a tree or window ornament.

On the blue sachet shown on page 72, the author used Appleton crewel wool thread in colors 912, 893, 744, and 461.

MASON JAR
SOFT TOPS

Crewelwork set into the metal lids of classic Mason jars? Why not! Fill the jars with jams and jellies–or with anything else you treasure.

PATTERNS

Puzzle Piece (see page 103)
Little Crown (see page 103)
Magic Ring (see page 103)

STITCHES

Satin Stitch,
French Knot

WHAT YOU NEED

White linen twill, 9 inches square (23 x 23 cm), one piece for each Mason jar soft top

Hoop, 5 inches (12.75 cm) in diameter

Crewel wool thread in the following colors:

Puzzle Piece: 1 skein each of light blue and chocolate brown

Little Crown: 1 skein each of orange and medium pink

Magic Ring: 1 skein each of dark orange and medium pink

Chenille needle, size 24, or comparable crewel needle of choice

3 Mason jars, any size (with tops that separate into two pieces, the band and lid)

6 cotton balls

Tracing paper

Fabric pen or pencil

Scissors

Craft glue that will dry clear

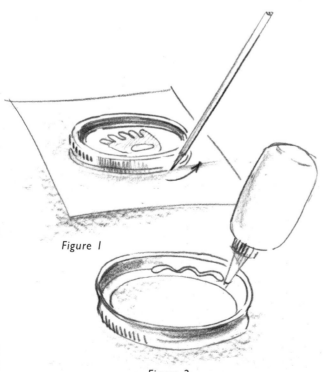

Figure 1

Figure 2

INSTRUCTIONS

1

Using the tracing paper and the fabric pen or pencil, transfer the designs onto the centers of the white linen twill squares (see page 19).

2

Hoop one piece of fabric, centering the design in the hoop (see page 19).

3

Embroider the design, using the colors and stitches indicated in the pattern diagram.

4

Block the finished crewelwork (see page 21).

5

Lay the finished crewelwork face up on a flat surface.

6

Center a band from a Mason jar top on top of the crewelwork.

7

Using your fabric pen or pencil, draw a circle on the fabric using the outer edge of the band as your guide (fig. 1).

8

Cut the circle out of the fabric along the line you've drawn.

9

Carefully pull apart two of the cotton balls and form a single ball approximately 1 1/2 inches (4 cm) around.

10

Put a line of glue on the top inside edge of the band (fig. 2).

11

Set the lid on the jar.

12

Put a line of glue on the top outer edge of the lid. Place the 1 1/2 inch (4 cm) ball of cotton on the lid. Center the fabric circle on top of the ball of cotton (fig. 3).

13

Carefully push the band (with glue along inner top edge) down over the fabric, and screw to the jar.

Figure 3

14

Let the jar sit for 15 minutes to dry before opening.

15

Repeat for the other two designs.

VARIATIONS

Omit the cotton balls for a lid that's not puffy.

If you're crafty enough to make your own jam and want to decorate the jar with a crewelwork top, skip steps 5 through 15. Instead, using pinking shears, trim your finished crewelwork to about 6 inches (15.25 cm) square or round and simply place between the lid and the band.

For Puzzle Piece, the author used Appleton crewel wool in colors 742 and 915.

For Little Crown, the author used Appleton crewel wool in colors 862 and 943.

For Magic Ring, the author used Appleton crewel wool in colors 864 and 943.

ELEGANT PILLOW
COVER

Make a gorgeous pillow for your bed or sofa with crewelwork
on the front and a coordinating fabric backing.

WHAT YOU NEED

White linen twill, 24 inches square (61 × 61 cm)

Hoop, 6 to 12 inches (15.25 to 30.5 cm) in diameter

Crewel wool thread, 1 skein each of light brown, light medium pink, medium pink, pink, and palest pink

Chenille needle, size 24, or comparable crewel needle of choice

White cotton fabric for lining, 1 piece 20 inches square (51 × 51 cm) and 2 pieces 16 × 20 inches (40.5 × 51 cm)

Coordinating fabric for pillow back, 2 pieces, each 16 × 20 inches (40.5 × 51 cm)

1 to 3 buttons, at least 3/4 inch (2 cm)

9 inches (23 cm) of 1/8-inch-wide (.5 cm) satin ribbon

Pillow form, 18 inches square (45.75 × 45.75 cm)

Copy machine or scanner to enlarge pattern

Tracing paper

Fabric pen or pencil

Scissors

Straight pins

Sewing thread

Hand sewing needle

INSTRUCTIONS

 1

Using the copy machine or scanner, enlarge the Balloon Drop pattern by 2 times and transfer the enlarged pattern onto the center of the white linen twill fabric (see page 19).

2

Starting with the top left section of the design, hoop a portion of the fabric (see page 19). Because this design is much larger than the hoop, you will need to work in sections, unscrewing the hoop and rehooping as you complete an area.

3

Embroider the outline of the design using Split Stitch.

4

Embroider the rest of the design, using colors and stitches as indicated in the Balloon Drop pattern diagram. For this design, wrap the thread around the needle four times for each French Knot Stalk.

5

Block your finished crewelwork (see page 21).

6

Trim 2 inches (5 cm) from each side of your embroidery, leaving a 1-inch (2.5 cm) border on all sides. The linen fabric with finished crewelwork should now measure 20 inches square (51 × 51 cm).

7

Lay your crewelwork face down on a flat surface. Place the piece of 20-inch-square (51 × 51 cm) lining fabric on top of your crewelwork. Pin the two pieces of fabric together and baste with the sewing thread and hand sewing needle, using a series of long, 1 to 2 inch (2.5 to 5 cm) straight stitches in diagonal rows spaced about 3 inches (7.5 cm) apart (fig. 1). Don't make these stitches too tight, since you'll remove them later.

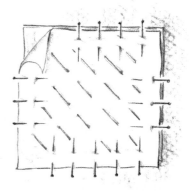

Figure 1

PATTERN

Balloon Drop (see page 105)

STITCHES

Chain Stitch,
Blanket Stitch,
Split Stitch,
French Knot Stalk

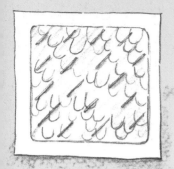

Figure 2

Figure 3

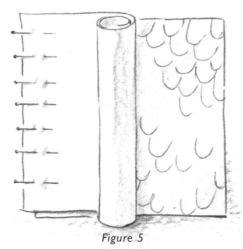

Figure 4

80

8

Using the sewing thread and hand sewing needle, and working on the front side of your crewelwork, make a line of Back Stitch parallel and very close to the outer edge of the Split Stitch crewel outline (fig. 2). Set aside.

9

Lay one of the 16 x 20 (40.5 x 51 cm) pillow back pieces of fabric face down on a flat surface. Place one of the 16 x 20 inch (40.5 x 51 cm) pieces of lining fabric on top of the pillow back fabric. Pin together and baste as described above. Repeat for the second piece of pillow back and lining fabric.

10

For each pillow back piece, fold one long edge 2 inches (5 cm) in toward the lining. Press with a hot iron, or form a crease by rubbing your fingers along the fold. Fold again another 2 inches (5 cm), press or crease with fingers, and pin along the folded edge (fig. 3).

11

Using your sewing thread, run a line of Blanket Stitch along the inside folded edge on each of the pieces (fig. 4). Remove the pins. You should now have two 12 x 20-inch (30.5 x 51 cm) pieces of basted, lined, and hemmed fabric that will be used to make the backing for your pillow.

12

Lay your basted and lined crewelwork face up on a flat surface. Lay one of the small pieces face down on top

Figure 5

of the crewelwork, with the fold in the middle and the left side edges lining up (fig. 5). Pin the left side edges together. Lay the other small piece in the same manner, matched to the right side edge of the crewelwork, and pin the right side edges. The two folded and hemmed edges now overlap in the center (fig. 6).

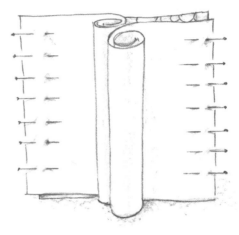

Figure 6

13

Pin the top and bottom edges, and place a few pins through the center, where the two smaller pieces overlap. Flip your work so that the lining side of the crewelwork is facing up.

14

Using the sewing thread and Back Stitch, and following the line of Back Stitch you made in step 8, sew the three pieces together in a seam around all four edges, sewing right on top of the first row of Back Stitch.

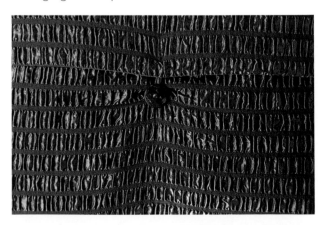

15

Remove all of the pins.

16

Trim the seam allowances to ½ inch (1.25 cm).

17

Trim corners, being careful not to cut through the stitching (fig. 7).

Figure 7

18

Remove the basting stitches.

19

Turn the pillow right side out.

20

Using the end of a blunt scissors, knitting needle, or chopstick, gently push out corners. Be careful not to push too hard, or you'll poke a hole in your work.

21

With the fabric pen, mark a spot in the center of the back of the pillow on the folded edge where a button will go. Stitch the button in place. If desired, add two more buttons, each about 4 inches (10 cm) equidistant from the first.

22

Fold a piece of ribbon in half and pin to the inside of the upper pillow flap with just enough hanging out to loop around the button (fig. 8). Stitch in place. If you've used additional buttons, add ribbon loops for those as well.

Figure 8

23

Slip your pillow into the opening of your pillow cover, adjust, and button up. Toss the pillow on your couch and lay your head to rest—you've earned it!

VARIATIONS

Instead of a coordinating fabric, back the pillow using the same white linen twill that you use for crewelwork.

Increase or decrease the design size to fit any pillow.

The author used Appleton crewel wool in colors 912, 942, 943, 944, and 751.

LAVENDER EYE
PILLOW

**Soothe your senses with this hand-embroidered
lavender eye pillow.**

WHAT YOU NEED

White linen twill, 10 x 14 inches (25.5 x 35.5 cm)

Hoop, 6 inches (15.25 cm) in diameter

Crewel wool thread, 1 skein each of light brown, olive brown, periwinkle blue, lavender, and palest periwinkle blue

Chenille needle, size 24, or comparable crewel needle of choice

Complementary fabric for backing, preferably a washable silk or another medium-weight, natural fabric, 6 x 9 ½ inches (15.25 x 24 cm)

1 ½ cups dried lavender

Tracing paper

Fabric pen or pencil

Scissors

Straight pins

Sewing thread

Hand sewing needle

INSTRUCTIONS

1

Trace two copies of the Wild Bunch pattern. With a scissors, cut off the border on the left edge of one copy, and the border on the right edge of the other. Tape the two copies together at the trimmed edges to make a pattern that is now 3 x 6 inches (7.5 x 15.25 cm). Using a copy machine, enlarge the design by 133 percent to 4 x 8 inches (10 x 20.25 cm).

2

Now using the tracing paper and fabric pen or pencil, transfer this enlarged design onto the center of the white linen twill (see page 19).

3

Hoop the linen twill fabric, centering the left half of the transferred design in the hoop (see page 19).

4

Embroider the outline of the design using Split Stitch. Unscrew and rehoop the fabric as necessary to work your way around the entire design.

5

Embroider the rest of design inside the Split Stitch outline, using colors and stitches as indicated in the Wild Bunch diagram.

6

Block your finished crewelwork (see page 21).

7

Trim 2 inches (5 cm) from each side of your embroidery, leaving a 1-inch (2.5 cm) border on all sides. Your fabric should now measure 6 x 10 inches (15.25 x 25.5 cm).

8

Lay the finished crewelwork face up on a flat surface.

9

Lay the backing fabric face down on top of the crewelwork (right sides together).

10

Pin the two pieces together on all edges.

11

With the sewing thread and hand sewing needle, using Back Stitch and stitching very close to and parallel to the Split Stitch outline of your crewelwork, stitch the two pieces together, leaving a 2-inch (5 cm) opening in the center of one of the short ends.

PATTERN

Wild Bunch (see page 107)

STITCHES

Split Stitch, Seed Stitch, Back Stitch

12

Remove all of the pins.

13

Trim the seam allowances to ⅜ inch (1 cm) on all sides.

14

Trim the corners.

15

Turn the eye pillow right side out through the opening.

16

Using the end of a blunt scissors, knitting needle, or chopstick, gently push out the corners. Be careful not to push too hard, or you'll poke a hole in your work.

17

Press the eye pillow with a warm iron.

18

Using a spoon or a funnel, pour the dried lavender into the opening. Don't overfill. Your eye pillow should be loose and floppy.

19

Fold in the remaining seam allowance at the opening, pin, and stitch closed.

The author used Appleton crewel wool in colors 912, 312, 893, 102, and 461.

SPARKLING
BLUE JEANS

Embroidered "sparkles" decorate the lower edge of a pair of blue jeans. This is a free-form project—because the fabric is dark, it's impossible to use the transferring technique used elsewhere, so you'll create the design yourself. Have fun!

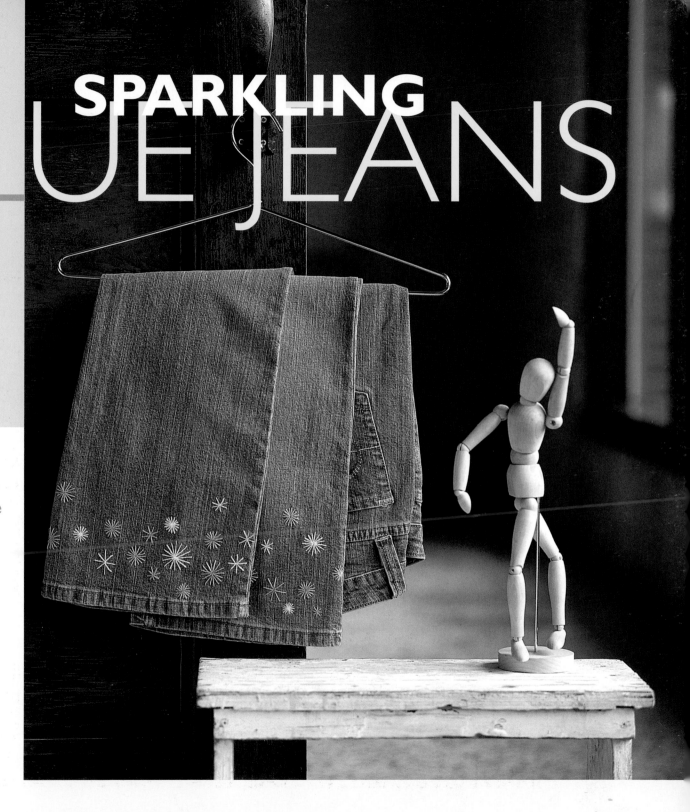

PATTERN

Variation of Cool Starbursts (see page 108)

STITCH

Variation of Spiderweb Stitch

WHAT YOU NEED

Hoop, 5 inches (12.75 cm) in diameter or smaller

Crewel wool thread, 1 skein each of palest periwinkle blue and white

Chenille needle, size 24, or comparable crewel needle of choice

Pair of blue jeans

Fabric pen

INSTRUCTIONS

1

Using the fabric pen, draw a sprinkling of dots randomly along the bottom edge of each pant leg, making sure to go all the way around each leg. You may draw out eight or 16 dots around the center dot, or just eyeball it as you work.

2

Hoop a portion of one pant leg to begin.

3

Make a knot in the end of your thread. In this project, unlike traditional crewel on linen, you must make a new knot in the end of your thread before beginning each sparkle. The knots won't show, since they are on the inside of the pant leg.

4

Embroider the design using Straight Stitch as it is used in the first half of the Spiderweb Stitch (see page 29). When making the spokes of the Spiderweb Stitch, always go DOWN through the same center point from the front of the fabric to the back of the fabric, and come UP to the outer points.

5

Make a knot at the completion of each sparkle, cutting your thread close to the knot, and begin a new sparkle with a knotted thread. Alternate between the white and blue threads as you work from one sparkle to the next. Vary the size of each sparkle, making some smaller and some larger. And remember to begin and end each sparkle with a new knot. This will help in the event that one of the sparkles wears out over time and the thread breaks—you will only lose one sparkle instead of all of them (and if you decide you'd like to remove one for design purposes, it's easy to do).

6

Unscrew and reposition your hoop as necessary until you have embroidered your way all the way around each pant leg.

7

There's no need to block, but if you like, give each pant leg a quick press with a warm iron. Be sure to wash your embroidered jeans in cold water, and line-dry. The wool crewel threads will shrink in warm water or in a hot dryer.

VARIATIONS

Add the full Spiderweb Stitch or Eyelet Holes to your design.

Work in beads or sequins to make your jeans really sparkle.

The author used Appleton crewel wool in colors 461 and 991.

EYELET HOLE
LAMPSHADE

Eyelet holes are fun to embroider, and make for a very luminous lampshade.

PATTERN

Variation of Falling Snow
(see page 110)

STITCHES

Eyelet Hole Stitch,
Blanket Stitch

WHAT YOU NEED

Wire lampshade frame

White linen twill (see instructions below to calculate the correct fabric measurements for your lampshade frame)

White cotton fabric for lining, in same amount as white linen twill

Hoop, 6 inches (15.25 cm) in diameter

Crewel wool thread, 2 skeins of white

Chenille needle, size 24, or comparable crewel needle of choice

Measuring tape

Scissors

Tracing paper

Fabric pen or pencil

Sewing thread to match linen fabric

Hand sewing needle

Straight pins

Note: Look for a wire lampshade frame at a hardware store or specialty lamp supply store, or tear off the fabric from an old lampshade and use that frame. Just be sure that top ring is wider than the base of the lamp (fig. 1).

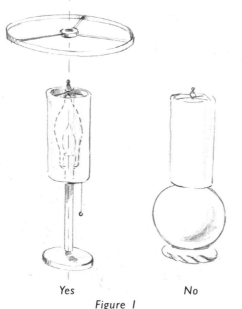

Yes   No

Figure 1

INSTRUCTIONS

1

Using the measuring tape, measure the circumference of the wire frame. Add 6 inches (15.25 cm) to that measurement. Decide how tall you want your shade to be, and add 4 inches (10 cm) to that measurement. This will be your fabric measurement. Cut the white linen twill fabric to this size. The completed shade shown in this project is 20 inches (51 cm) in circumference and 15 inches (38 cm) tall. Thus, the fabric was cut to 26 x 19 inches (66 x 48.25 cm).

2

For the dimensions of the lining fabric, subtract 1 inch (2.5 cm) from the width and $2\frac{1}{4}$ inches from the height of the linen fabric. The lining fabric for the lampshade shown was cut to 25 x $16\frac{3}{4}$ inches (63.5 x 42.5 cm).

3

Using the tracing paper and the fabric pen or pencil, transfer the Falling Snow design onto the lower edge of the linen fabric, allowing for a 3-inch (7.5 cm) hem on the lower edge and sides. Repeat until the design covers the lower edge (see page 19 for transferring tips).

4

Hoop the fabric, centering the circles in the hoop (see page 19).

5

Using Eyelet Hole Stitch, embroider each hole. Unscrew and rehoop your fabric as necessary to work your way around the entire edge of the shade.

6

Block your finished crewelwork (see page 21).

7

Trim 2 inches (5 cm) from the lower edge and each of the two sides of your embroidery, leaving a 1-inch (2.5 cm) border on these three sides.

8

Fold the embroidered linen in half, right sides together, and pin the side edges together (fig. 2). With the sewing thread and hand sewing needle, using Back Stitch, sew the pinned edges in a seam exactly 1 inch (2.5 cm) from the edge, making a tube. Press the seam open with a warm iron.

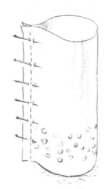

Figure 2

9

Turn under a ¼-inch (1 cm) hem on the lower edge of the embroidered linen, then fold again ¼ inch (1 cm). Pin the hem in place. Using the sewing thread and hand sewing needle, hem the shade, using a basic hemstitch or a short Blanket Stitch. Remove the pins. Press the hemmed lower edge with a warm iron (fig. 3).

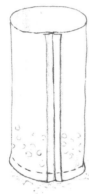

Figure 3

10

Repeat steps 8 and 9 with the lining fabric.

11

Turn the linen tube right side out.

12

Fit the lining tube into the linen tube, wrong sides together, lining up the top edges. Pin the top edges together and baste with a row of Straight Stitch.

13

With the frame attached to the lamp and the lamp set on a table, place the embroidered shade around the wire frame.

14

With your fabric pen, make a mark at each wire cross-bar of the frame. With your scissors, make 1-inch (2.5 cm) snips in the top edge of the fabric tube at each of these three marks.

15

With the slits lined up with the wire cross bars, roll about 1 inch (2.5 cm) of the upper edge of the shade over the wire frame toward the inside. Pin and stitch in place using a basic hemstitch (fig. 4).

16

Turn on the light and admire!

VARIATION

Repeat the pattern over the whole shade, top to bottom, or make up your own design using the Eyelet Hole Stitch.

The author used Appleton crewel wool in color 991.

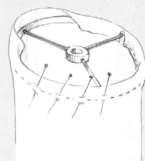

Figure 4

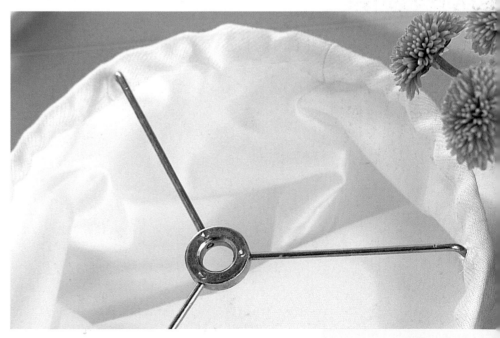

WHIMSICAL EYEGLASS CASE

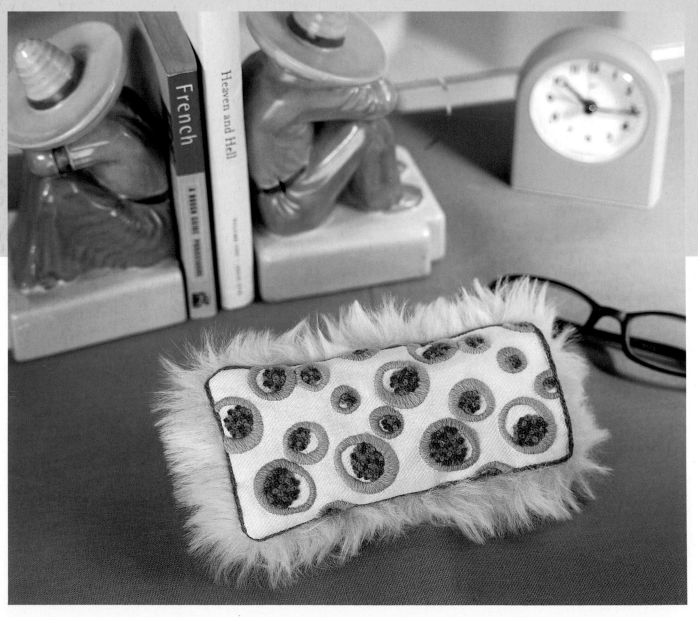

Keep your eyeglasses safe in a visually exciting case backed with fake fur.

WHAT YOU NEED

White linen twill, 10 x 14 inches (25.5 x 35.5 cm)

Hoop, 6 inches (15.25 cm) in diameter

Chenille needle, size 22, or comparable crewel needle of choice

Crewel wool thread, 1 skein each of sky blue, light blue-green, orange, bright yellow-orange, bright orange, dark orange, and light brown

Piece of aqua blue faux fur, fleece, or similar fuzzy fabric, 6 x 12 inches (15.25 x 30.5 cm)

Copy machine to enlarge design

Tracing paper

Fabric pen or pencil

Scissors

Tape

Straight pins

Sewing thread

Hand sewing needle

INSTRUCTIONS

1

Trace two copies of the Dinner Party pattern. With scissors, cut off the border on the left edge of one copy, and the border on the right edge of the other. Tape the two copies together at the trimmed edges to make a pattern that is now 3 x 6 inches (7.5 x 15.25 cm). Using a copy machine, enlarge the design by 133 percent to 4 x 8 inches (10 x 20.25 cm).

2

Now, using the tracing paper and fabric pen or pencil, transfer this enlarged design onto the center of the white linen twill (see page 19).

3

Hoop the linen twill, centering the left half of the design in the hoop (see page 19).

4

Embroider the outline of the design using two rows of Split Stitch. Unscrew and move your hoop as necessary to work your way across the entire design.

5

Embroider the rest of the design with Satin Stitch and French Knot, using the colors and stitches indicated in the Dinner Party diagram.

6

Block your finished crewelwork (see page 21).

7

Trim 2 inches from the two long sides and one of the short sides of your embroidered linen. Leave the other short side untrimmed (fig. 1). Your fabric should now measure 6 x 12 inches (15.25 x 30.5 cm).

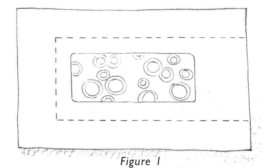

Figure 1

8

Lay the finished crewelwork face up on a flat surface. Lay the faux fur fabric face down on top of the crewelwork (right sides together), lining up all the edges. Pin the two pieces together (fig. 2).

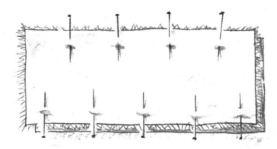

Figure 2

PATTERN

Variation of Dinner Party (see page 102)

STITCHES

Split Stitch, Satin Stitch, French Knot

9

With the sewing thread and the hand-sewing needle, use Back Stitch to sew a 1-inch (2.5 cm) seam on both long sides and the trimmed short side. The seamline should be very close to, and parallel to, the outer edge of the Split Stitch outline of your crewelwork. Leave the untrimmed edge open.

10

Remove the pins.

11

Trim the stitched seams to ⅜ inch (1 cm) on all sides except the open edge. Trim the corners (fig. 3).

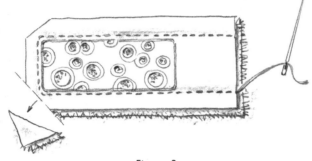

Figure 3

12

Turn the eyeglass case right side out. Using the end of a blunt scissors, knitting needle, or chopstick, gently push out the corners. Be careful not to push too hard or you'll poke a hole in your work.

13

Fold the excess fabric on the open end of the eyeglass case to the inside of the case, bringing it even with the edge of the embroidery.

14

With a few tiny stitches, tack this folded edge to the inside of the case at the side seams.

15

If you like, make a tiny row of Straight Stitch next to the Split Stitch outline on the folded edge of the opening.

VARIATIONS

Resize the design and make a case for your digital music player, cell phone, or camera.

Make a shoulder strap by stitching a ribbon to the side seams on the open end.

The author used Appleton crewel wool in colors 561, 522, 862, 556, 442, 864, and 912.

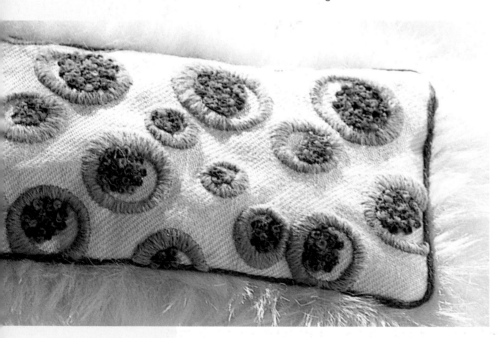

HAUTE-COUTURE
APRON

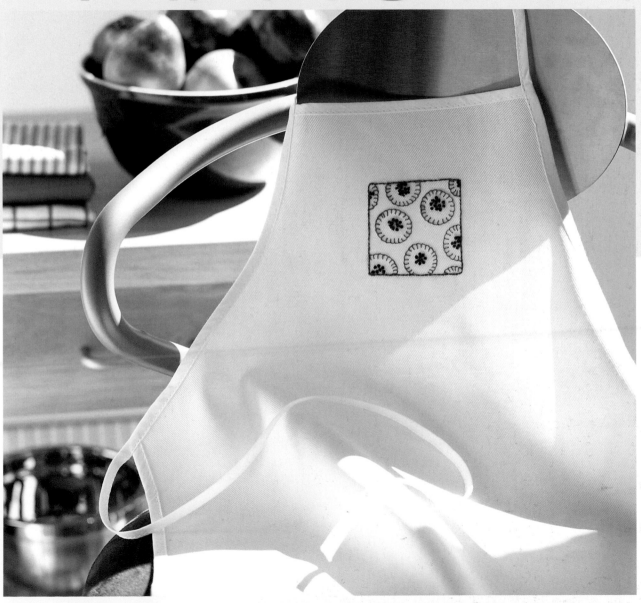

For your favorite stylish chef, embroider a bright crewelwork
design directly onto the bib of a crisp white apron.

PATTERN

Raspberry Treats (see page 107)

STITCHES

Blanket Stitch,
French Knot,
Split Stitch

WHAT YOU NEED

White chef's apron

Hoop, 6 inches (15.25 cm) in diameter

Crewel wool thread, 1 skein each of periwinkle blue, deep pink and light brown

Chenille needle, size 24, or comparable crewel needle of choice

Tracing paper

Fabric pen or pencil

INSTRUCTIONS

1

Using the tracing paper and the fabric pen or pencil, transfer the Raspberry Treats design to the center of the bib of the apron (see page 19).

2

Hoop the fabric, centering the design in the hoop (see page 19).

3

Embroider the design, using the stitches and colors indicated in the Raspberry Treats diagram.

4

Block the finished crewelwork (see page 21).

5

Get cookin'!

VARIATIONS

Embroider the name of the chef below the design.

Make a matching chef's hat.

The author used Appleton crewel wool in colors 893, 946, and 912.

SKIRT EMBELLISHMENT

Enhance a knee-length wool skirt with crewel embroidery on the bottom edge.

PATTERN

Inspired by Ruby Shoots
(see page 104)

STITCH

Split Stitch

WHAT YOU NEED

Wool skirt

Hoop, 6 inches (15.25 cm) in diameter

Crewel wool thread, 5 skeins of sky blue

Chenille needle, size 22, or comparable crewel needle of choice

Fabric pen (the vanishing kind)

INSTRUCTIONS

1

Lay your skirt on a flat surface and smooth out all the wrinkles.

2

Using the vanishing fabric pen, draw a row of curly "shoots" varying in size from 2 to 4 inches (5 to 10 cm) and spaced at least ¾ inch (2 cm) above the lower edge of the skirt, all the way around. Don't try to make them perfect. Their simple randomness will be refreshing!

3

Hoop a portion of the skirt's edge.

4

Knot and thread your needle and begin embroidering using Split Stitch. Make each "shoot" with two rows of Split Stitch.

5

Unscrew and rehoop your fabric as you finish one area and move onto the next.

6

After completing the entire row, press the skirt with a warm iron (not too hot—wool is sensitive).

VARIATION

Try the same design on the edge of a jacket, shirt, or dress.

The author used Appleton crewel wool in color 561.

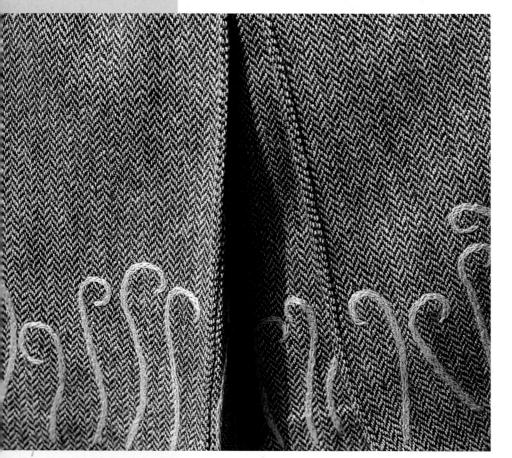

COZY
SCARF

Bundle up and stay warm with a fleece scarf in a bright color—
the perfect backdrop for crewel embroidery with tapestry wool thread,
which is slightly heavier than crewel wool.

PATTERN

Inspired by Scarlet Sparks
(see page 107)

STITCH

Variation of
Spiderweb Stitch

WHAT YOU NEED

Red fleece fabric, 60 × 15 inches (152 × 38 cm)

Hoop, 6 inches (15.25 cm) in diameter, or larger

Tapestry wool thread, 2 skeins of sky blue

Tapestry needle, size 18 or 20

Scissors

Fabric pen

Straight pins

Sewing thread to match fabric

Hand sewing needle

INSTRUCTIONS

1

Lay your fabric on a flat surface and smooth out the
wrinkles with your hands.

2

With the scissors, cut 2½ inch (6.5 cm) slits at ½-inch
(1.25 cm) intervals along each end for fringe.

3

Using the fabric pen, draw about 14 dots randomly
along each end of the fabric rectangle, spacing the dots
approximately 3 inches (7.5 cm) apart and at least 1
inch (2.5 cm) from where the fringe begins.

4

Hoop a portion of the fabric on one end. Don't tighten
too much or you'll crush the fuzziness of the fabric.

5

Using the tapestry needle and knotted thread, embroider the design using your drawn dots as the centers of
each Spiderweb (see page 29). Unlike traditional crewel
on linen, you should start and end each Spiderweb with
a knot. Note: For this design, the Spiderwebs are only
partially completed, allowing the spokes of the web to
stick out.

6

Unscrew and reposition your hoop as necessary until
you have embroidered all of the Spiderwebs on both
ends of the scarf (fig. 1).

Figure 1

7

Fold the fabric lengthwise with right sides together (the
front of the crewelwork on the inside). Pin the long
edge and sew the seam, using Back Stitch, with the
hand sewing needle and sewing thread (fig. 2). Remove
the pins and turn the scarf right side out.

Figure 2

8

Lay the scarf flat, with the seam along one edge. Pin
and stitch each end closed where the fringe meets
the scarf (fig. 3). Remove the pins.

Figure 3

9

Dry clean, or wash in cold water and line dry.

**The author used Appleton tapestry wool in
color 561.**

ADORNED MESH BAG

Crewel embroidery makes a plain mesh zipper bag anything but ordinary.
I found this orange bag at a little gift shop, and adapted a favorite
crewel pattern to complement its bright color.

PATTERN

Tulip Tops with color variation—instead of a brown border, substitute a vivid orange (see page 104)

STITCHES

Split Stitch,
Satin Stitch

WHAT YOU NEED

Mesh bag, any size—ours is 8 × 10 inches (20.25 × 25.5 cm)

Crewel wool thread, 1 skein each of bright orange, pale orange, medium pink, and pink

Chenille needle, size 24, or comparable crewel needle of choice

Tracing paper (or copy machine)

Fabric pen

Tape

INSTRUCTIONS

1

Make a copy of the Tulip Tops pattern using a copy machine, or transfer the design to a piece of paper using the tracing paper and marker or pencil.

2

Tape the copied or transferred pattern to the inside of the mesh bag, facing out, and trace it with your fabric pen. You should be able to see the design through the mesh.

3

Don't bother trying to hoop the mesh. Mesh is made of plastic, and fairly rigid. It should hold its shape enough to embroider on it. Hooping it could bend the mesh permanently—not good.

4

Make a knot in the end of your thread, and embroider the outline of the design using Split Stitch.

5

Embroider the rest of the design inside the Split Stitch outline using the colors and stitches indicated in the Tulip Tops diagram, substituting bright orange for brown. **Note:** Be sure not to run a thread from one shape to another, as it will show through the mesh.

VARIATION

If you don't find an orange mesh bag like the one shown, simply change the suggested thread colors in this design to match your mesh bag.

If you find a larger bag, such as a mesh shopping bag with handles, try enlarging or repeating a design multiple times.

The author used Appleton crewel wool in colors 442, 622, 943, and 944.

THE NEW CREWEL PATTERN DIAGRAMS

NEW CREWEL CIRCLE SAMPLER

white Split
Stitch outline

white Stem Stitch

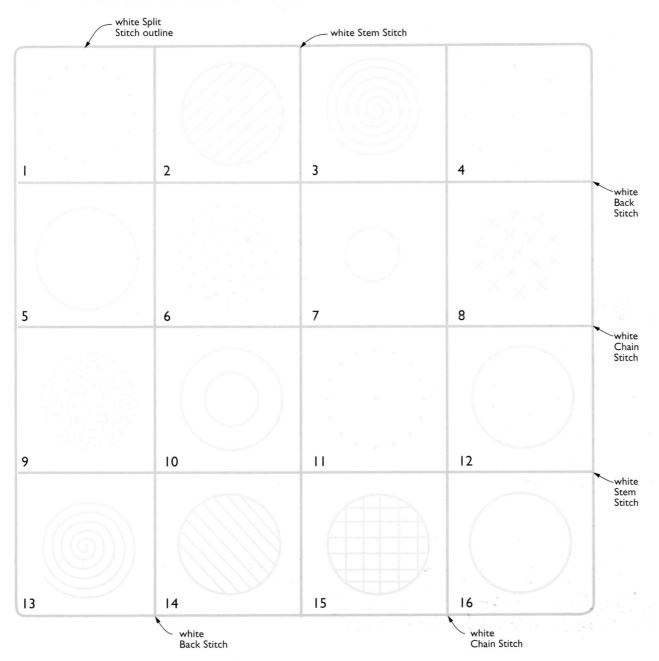

white
Back
Stitch

white
Chain
Stitch

white
Stem
Stitch

white
Back Stitch

white
Chain Stitch

page 33

use pale yellow-green
for #1-13 & #16

1. Straight Stitch
2. Satin Stitch
3. Back Stitch
4. Spiderweb Stitch
5. Chain Stitch
6. French Knot
7. Eyelet Hole Stitch
8. Cross Stitch
   French Knot
9. Seed Stitch
10. Split Stitch
11. French Knot Stalks
12. Blanket Stitch
13. Stem Stitch
14. Soft Shading
15. Square Filling Stitch
16. Overcast Stitch

#14: use white, cream
white, and pale yellow-green

#15: use pale yellow-green
for the split stitch outline
and the short straight
stitches; use white for the
long straight stitches

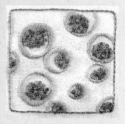

page 37

page 38

page 39

SNOW SHOES

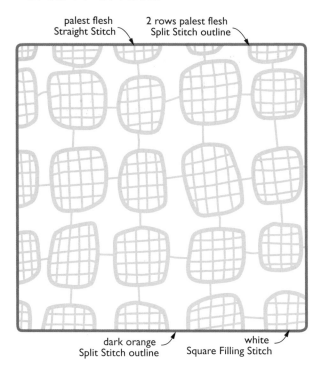

palest flesh
Straight Stitch

2 rows palest flesh
Split Stitch outline

dark orange
Split Stitch outline

white
Square Filling Stitch

MOON ROCK

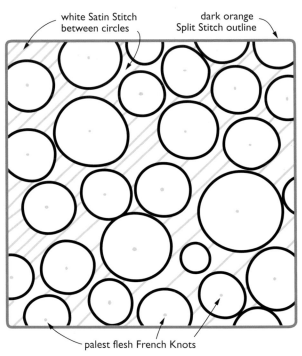

white Satin Stitch
between circles

dark orange
Split Stitch outline

palest flesh French Knots

DINNER PARTY

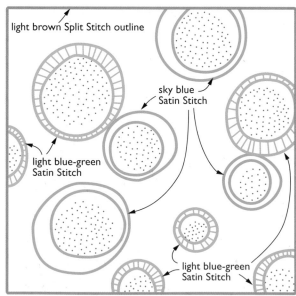

light brown Split Stitch outline

sky blue
Satin Stitch

light blue-green
Satin Stitch

light blue-green
Satin Stitch

⬚ ← orange, bright yellow-orange, bright orange French Knots

HIP SQUARES

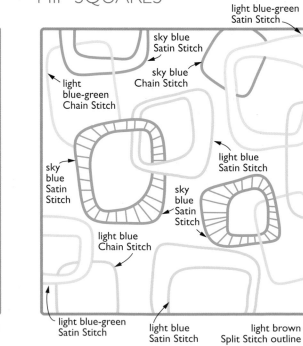

light blue-green
Satin Stitch

sky blue
Satin Stitch

sky blue
Chain Stitch

light
blue
Chain
Stitch

light
blue-green
Chain Stitch

light blue
Satin Stitch

sky
blue
Satin
Stitch

sky
blue
Satin
Stitch

light
blue-
green
Chain
Stitch

light blue
Chain Stitch

light blue-green
Satin Stitch

light blue
Satin Stitch

light brown
Split Stitch outline

PUZZLE PIECE

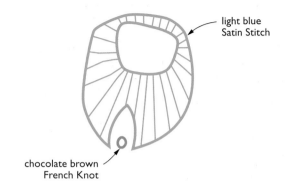

light blue
Satin Stitch

chocolate brown
French Knot

LITTLE CROWN

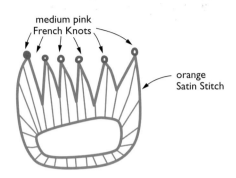

medium pink
French Knots

orange
Satin Stitch

MAGIC RING

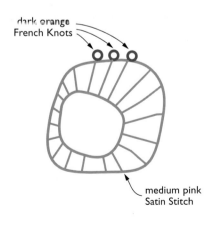

dark orange
French Knots

medium pink
Satin Stitch

DAISY BLUES

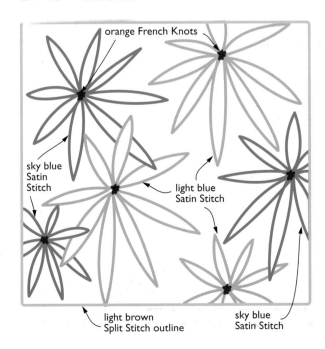

orange French Knots

sky blue
Satin
Stitch

light blue
Satin Stitch

light brown
Split Stitch outline

sky blue
Satin Stitch

page 40

page 41

page 42

page 43

103

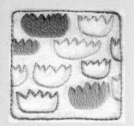

page 44

page 46

page 47

page 48

TULIP TOPS

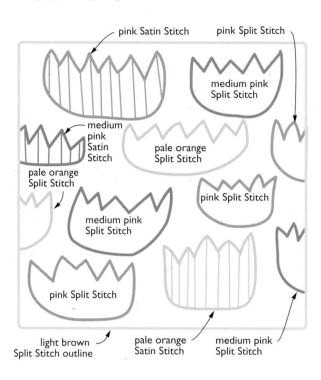

pink Satin Stitch

pink Split Stitch

medium pink
Split Stitch

medium pink Satin Stitch

pale orange Split Stitch

pale orange Split Stitch

medium pink Split Stitch

pink Split Stitch

pink Split Stitch

light brown Split Stitch outline

pale orange Satin Stitch

medium pink Split Stitch

CHAINLINK PINK

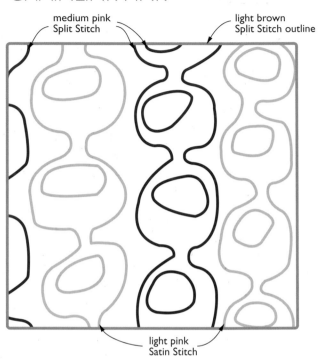

medium pink Split Stitch

light brown Split Stitch outline

light pink Satin Stitch

LOVE LOOPS

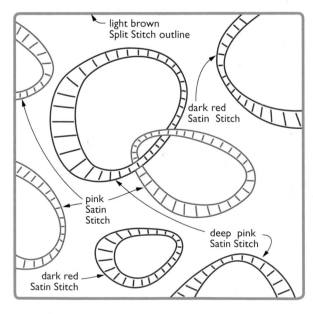

light brown Split Stitch outline

dark red Satin Stitch

pink Satin Stitch

deep pink Satin Stitch

dark red Satin Stitch

RUBY SHOOTS

dark red Split Stitch

light brown Split Stitch outline

BALLOON DROP

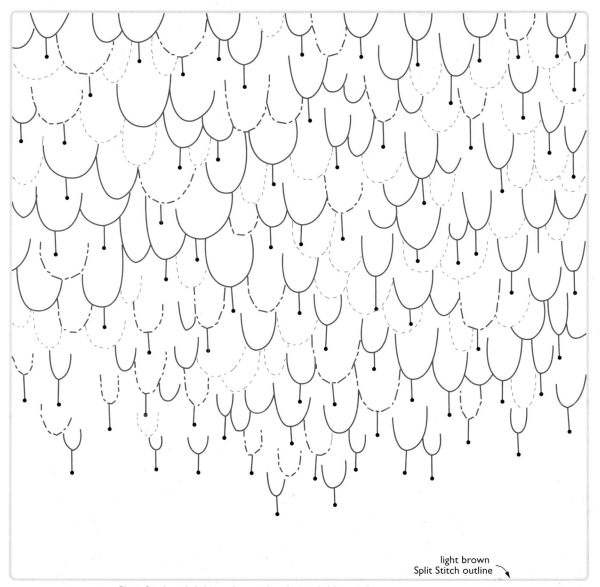

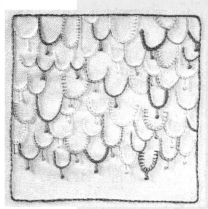

page 45

light brown
Split Stitch outline

—— Chain Stitch pink, light medium pink, palest pink (alternate)
– – Blanket Stitch pink, light medium pink, palest pink (alternate)
---- Split Stitch medium pink

SWAY DAYS

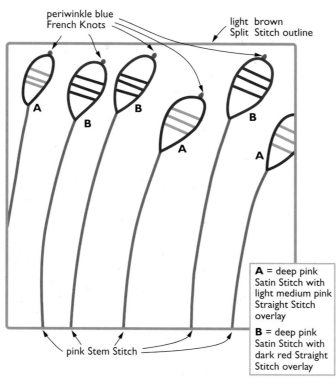

periwinkle blue
French Knots

light brown
Split Stitch outline

A

B
B

A

B

A

A = deep pink
Satin Stitch with
light medium pink
Straight Stitch
overlay

B = deep pink
Satin Stitch with
dark red Straight
Stitch overlay

pink Stem Stitch

SWEETHEART GARLAND

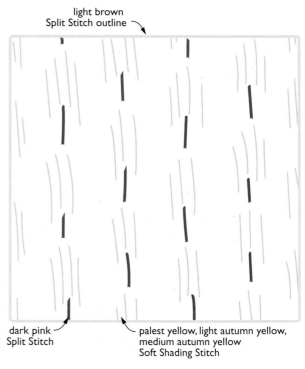

light brown
Split Stitch outline

dark pink
Split Stitch

palest yellow, light autumn yellow,
medium autumn yellow
Soft Shading Stitch

SPRING FLING

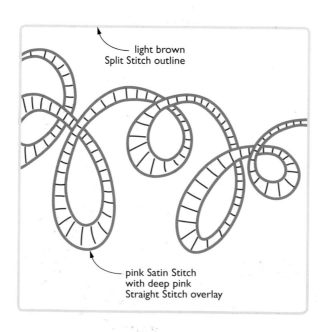

light brown
Split Stitch outline

pink Satin Stitch
with deep pink
Straight Stitch overlay

BLUE AGAVE

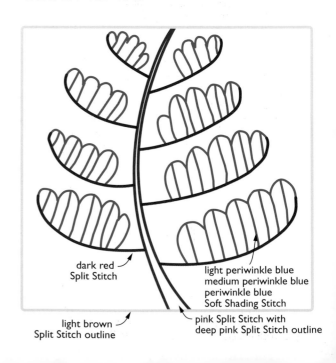

dark red
Split Stitch

light periwinkle blue
medium periwinkle blue
periwinkle blue
Soft Shading Stitch

pink Split Stitch with
deep pink Split Stitch outline

light brown
Split Stitch outline

SCARLET SPARKS

light brown
Split Stitch outline

alternate: Straight stitch spokes in dark red, weave in pink,
with Straight Stitch spokes in pink, weave in dark red

RASPBERRY TREATS

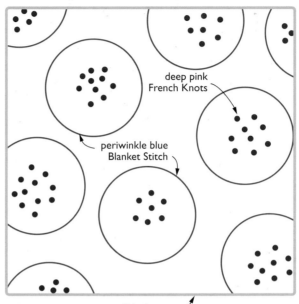

deep pink
French Knots

periwinkle blue
Blanket Stitch

light brown
Split Stitch outline

WILD BUNCH

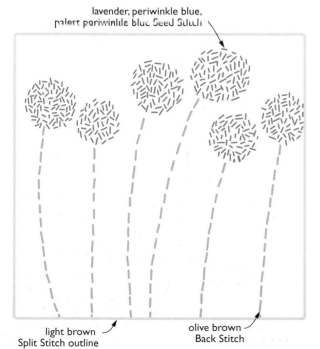

lavender, periwinkle blue,
palest periwinkle blue Seed Stitch

light brown
Split Stitch outline

olive brown
Back Stitch

SWEET BUTTONS

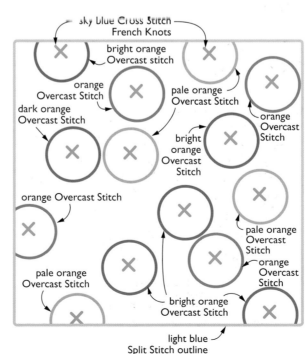

sky blue Cross Stitch
French Knots

bright orange
Overcast stitch

orange
Overcast Stitch

pale orange
Overcast Stitch

dark orange
Overcast Stitch

orange
Overcast
Stitch

bright
orange
Overcast
Stitch

orange Overcast Stitch

pale orange
Overcast
Stitch

orange
Overcast
Stitch

pale orange
Overcast Stitch

bright orange
Overcast Stitch

light blue
Split Stitch outline

page 53

page 54

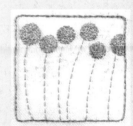

page 56

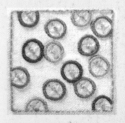

page 60

COOL STARBURSTS

light brown
Split Stitch outline

FISHING NET

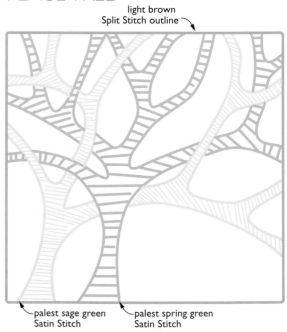

white Overcast Stitch

dark orange
Split Stitch
outline

palest
flesh
Overca
Stitch

white
Overcast Stitch

palest flesh Overcast Stitch

BIRTHDAY WISH

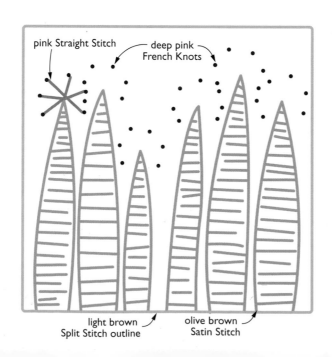

pink Straight Stitch

deep pink
French Knots

light brown
Split Stitch outline

olive brown
Satin Stitch

PEACE TREE

light brown
Split Stitch outline

palest sage green
Satin Stitch

palest spring green
Satin Stitch

QUEEN'S LACE

light brown
Split Stitch outline

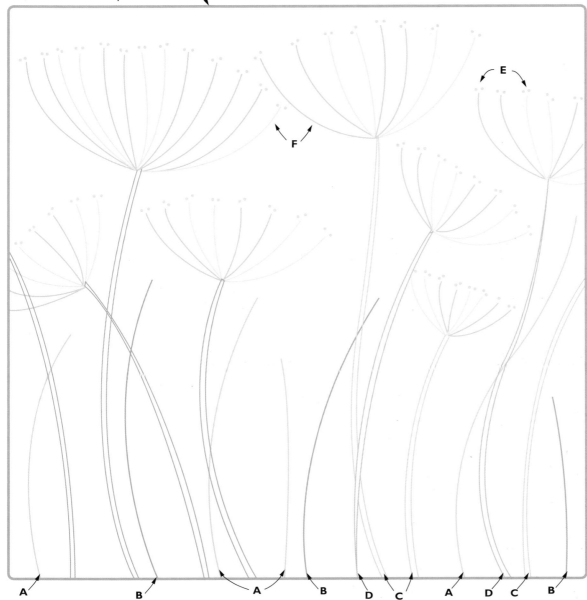

E

F

page 59

A   B   A   B   D C   A   D C   B

A light sage green
Stem Stitch

B spring green
Stem Stitch

C light spring green
Chain stitch

D medium spring green
Chain Stitch

E alternate
palest flesh and
white French Knots

F alternate
light spring green and
palest sage green
Split Stitch

FALLING SNOW

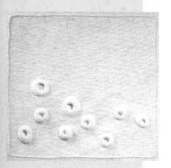

page 34

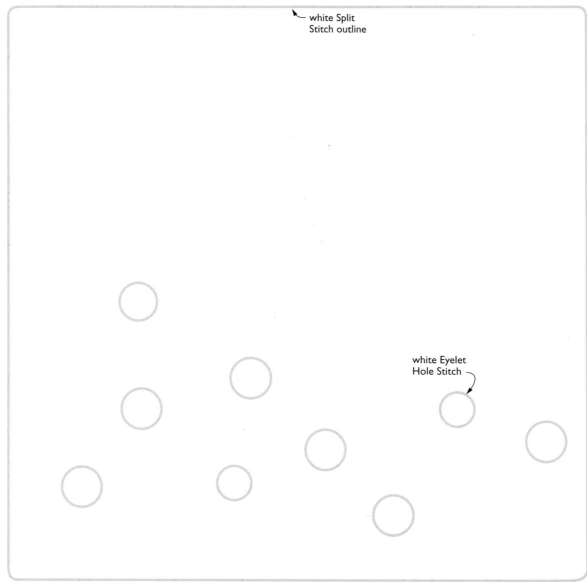

white Split
Stitch outline

white Eyelet
Hole Stitch

STARFISH

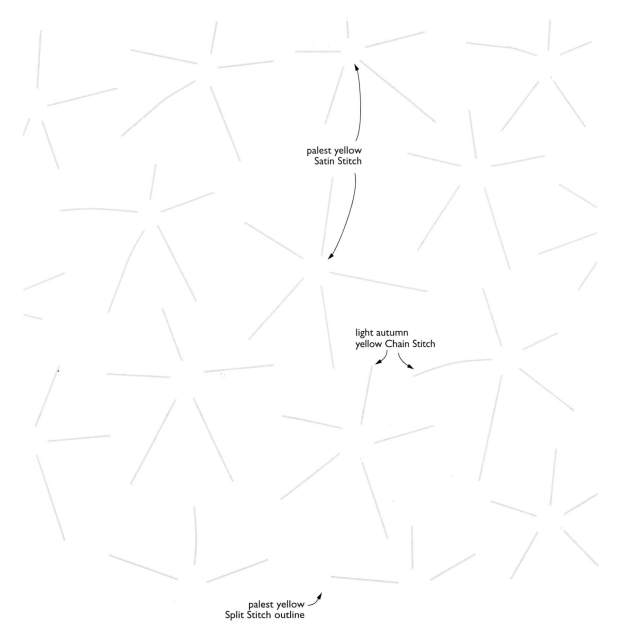

palest yellow
Satin Stitch

light autumn
yellow Chain Stitch

palest yellow
Split Stitch outline

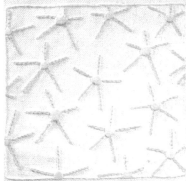

page 62

page 61

A palest yellow
Satin Stitch

B light autumn
yellow Satin Stitch

C medium autumn
yellow Satin Stitch

D palest sage green
Satin Stitch

E palest spring green
Satin Stitch

F medium blue/green
Satin Stitch

BABY GREENS

light brown
Split Stitch outline

C E B F A   D F D E A   F E F B   D

ACKNOWLEDGMENTS

Many thanks to my crafty mother, Joanne Shaughnessy, who back in the 1970s introduced me to the fiber arts by way of crewel embroidery, and to Tom Michael, who several years ago encouraged me to return to those crewel roots and come up with fresh designs for a new generation. Thanks also to the friends and family who have generously assisted me with my crewel intentions: Pia Bose, Anita Woolf, Dave Kajganich, Mary and Michael Claffey, Erin Zuiker, Roy Hamric, Brigid McDermott, Maureen Michael, The Big Guy, and the Crewel Girls: Haley, Claudia, Livia, and Lia. And a special thanks to Erica Wilson, the 20th century crewel pioneer, who through her many books and classes, perfected and popularized several of the stitches included in this book.

NOTES ABOUT SUPPLIERS

Usually, the supplies you need for making the projects in Lark books can be found at your local craft supply store, discount mart, home improvement center, or retail shop relevant to the topic of the book. Occasionally, however, you may need to buy materials or tools from specialty suppliers. In order to provide you with the most up-to-date information, we have created a listing of suppliers on our Web site, which we update on a regular basis. Visit us at www.larkbooks.com, click on "Craft Supply Sources," and then click on the relevant topic. You will find numerous companies listed with their web address and/or mailing address and phone number.